S0-AAE-496

MARK ALMOND

UPRISING!

Political Upheavals that have Shaped the World

BARNES
& NOBLE
BOOKS
NEW YORK

First published in 2002 by Mitchell Beazley,
an imprint of Octopus Publishing Group Ltd,

Executive Editors: Vivien Antwi and Lindsay Porter
Executive Art Editors: Christine Keilty and Kenny Grant
Project Editors: Naomi Waters and Michelle Bernard
Editor: Mary Loebig Giles
Design: Alexa Brommer
Production: Catherine Lay and Alex Wiltshire
Picture Research: Jenny Faithfull
Proofreader: Laura Harper
Indexer: Diane le Core

All rights reserved. No part of this work may be reproduced or utilized in any
form or by any means, electronic or mechanical, including photocopying, recording
or by any information storage and retrieval system, without the prior written
permission of the publisher.

This edition published by Barnes & Noble, Inc., by arrangement
with Mitchell Beazley

2002 Barnes & Noble Books

M 1 0 9 8 7 6 5 4 3 2 1

ISBN 0 7607 3348 1
A CIP catalogue record for this book is available from the British Library.

Typeset in Lucida, DIN Engschrift Alternate and Gill Sans.

Printed in China by Toppan Printing Company Ltd.

UPRISING!

contents

Introduction

Why do people revolt? What are the roots of revolution? How do some uprisings succeed in overturning society while others fail? Civil Discontent is as old as human society. History has been punctuated by uprisings. Injustice and ambition have fed the urge to transform society. For most of recorded history, the vast majority of humankind have been peasants toiling for the benefit of a few masters. Once the demands of the local lord were satisfuedm there was little left to meet their own basic needs. Yet revolt rarely led to fundamental change. Uprisings pock mark history as do their frequently brutal suppressions, but successful revolutions were rare until modern times.

THE SEX OF POLITICS

Successful revolutions are among the most dramatic and powerful developments in our past. It is only in recent centuries that sudden and complete breakdowns of a political system have opened the way to social upheaval and a transformation of the socio-economic order from below. To justify the name, a revolution must do more than change the personnel at the top or extend participation in a political system; it has to sweep away the old regime in politics, society, and the economy. Evolutionary change, in society as in nature, may well produce fundamental alterations over time, but revolutions are not gradual; they resemble sudden leaps.

War and foreign conquest have often produced similar results but nothing is more dramatic than an internal upheaval which shatters the social order and remodels it. What makes these uprisings possible is faith in the possibility of successful change. Even ostensibly atheist revolutionary movements like Communism in the twentieth century have relied on instilling a quasi-religious commitment and willingness for self-sacrifice in their supporters. In many ways, the spread of revolutionary ideals like those of the French Revolution or Russian Revolution resembles the tidal wave of early Islamic conversion in the seventh century. No-one should need reminding today that Islam still has enormous potential to appeal to self-sacrifice for the cause of transforming society's way of life. Unbelievers in either religion or ideology risk dismissing fanaticism as absurd. History is full of its triumphs and the defeat of sweet reason.

Revolutionary hopes have all too frequently given way to tragedy and bitter disappointment. Karl Marx's closest collaborator among the early Communists , Friedrich Engels, recognised the potential irony of his own project: "People who boast that they have made a revolution always realize the next day that they did not know

MADRID 1936

This 1936 photomontage by John Heartfield on the Spanish Civil War is entitled Madrid 1936 / No pasaran! Pasaremos! (They will not get through. We will get through!).

arm-in-arm in the streets to produce extraordinary results. In the mid-19th century, Karl Marx called revolutions the locomotives of history. So powerful is the allure of revolution that the American commentator, HL Mencken, called revolutions "the sex of politics". Whether we condone or condemn these uprisings, they exert an obligatory hold over our imaginations. And this is in spite of the fact that the word "revolution" has been debased by the tendency to call any change in some facet of society a revolution.

A RECENT PHENOMENON

There have been so many dramatic uprisings in recent centuries that it is easy to forget how recent in human history the idea of such upheavals has been. In ancient Greece, Aristotle and Plato analyzed how changes in economic conditions brought about changes in who ruled society, but ancient revolutions brought little fundamental change in the social or economic order. The position of the vast majority of the population – women and slaves of both sexes – was unaffected by changes at the top of society in the ancient world. Slave revolts, like that of Spartacus against Rome, and peasant revolts in feudal societies, whether like the Peasants' Revolt in medieval England in 1381 or the Taiping rebellion in mid-19th-century China, failed to alter the basic conditions of life. At best they undermined the stability of the political elite but did not achieve their own aims.

what they were doing, that the revolution they had made was quite different from the one they had intended to make."

Again and again, revolutionary ideals have turned sour on contact with reality, but the impulse to fundamental change has never died out – though its obituary has often been prematurely written.

Revolutions are fascinating to observe because they bring out, in the starkest possible fashion, the motive forces in history. Self-sacrifice and self- deception often march

Without an ideology to guide their struggle, primitive rebels usually had only short-sighted goals. As a riot briefly toppled the local authorities, they would ransack such hated institutions as tax offices or lynch their landlords' bailiffs. However, medieval rebels, for instance, were trapped by a deferential way of thinking even when they attacked their local oppressors. Invariably they believed in a powerful myth that their king was a benevolent and well-intentioned father figure who did not know how oppressive and greedy the nobility and his local representatives were. This naïve faith in the good-heartedness of the monarch was the downfall of many peasant revolts. As late as 1905 in Russia, this simple faith in the idea of a well-intentioned ruler misled by greedy and corrupt ministers was widespread and led to tragedy.

THE HOPE OF PROGRESS

In 1792, Thomas Paine described revolutions as sharp breaks in historical continuity. "What we formerly called revolutions were little more than a change of persons. But what we now see in the world, from the revolutions in America and France, are a renovations of the natural order of things, a system of principles as universal as truth and the existence of man, and combining moral and political happiness ad national prosperity." The idea of progress was a vital ingredient in the sucess of an uprising. As long as societies seemed stuck in fixed structures as if by nature or divine right, then the idea of fundamental change was difficult, probably impossible to conceive, certainly for most people.

The hope of progress was an important pre-condition for any successful revolution, but it also had to fall on fertile ground. As Trotsky noted, despair at hardship was not an ingredient for a successful revolution. Human history has been a history of drudgery for most people. For many, life is still too harsh a struggle for simple physical survival for there to be any energy left over for politics.

The French historian of revolution, Alexis de Tocqueville, noticed that when a despotic regime tried to reform itself, it often set off a chain reaction, leading to revolution by revealing hope to people who had previously been in despair: "Patiently endured so long as it seemed beyond redress, a grievance comes to appear intolerable once the possibility of removing it crosses men's minds." From the time of Louis XVI in France in the 1780s (about which Tocqueville was writing) to Mikhail Gorbachev's Soviet Union 200 years later, a regime's attempts to reform itself can trigger unrest and upheaval. Lenin recognised that the elite's loss of confidence was an essential condition: "For a revolution to take place, it is not enough for the exploited and oppressed masses to realize the impossibility of living in the old way; it is essential that the exploiters should not be able to live and rule in the old way. It is only when the 'lower classes' do not want to live in the old way and the 'upper classes' cannot carry on in the old way that the revolution can triumph."

TYPES OF REVOLUTION

Defining a great socio-political revolution is not an easy task, yet most people can recognize one when it occurs. They are like earthquakes with powerful aftershocks. The French Revolution of 1789 or the Russian Revolution in 1917 had reverberations in distant lands that previously knew little or nothing about France or Russia. Revolutions produce a kind of ideological electricity, transmitting ideas and slogans of protest across vast distances. Optimism is a key ingredient in any revolutionary upheaval. Without hope nothing can be changed.

What this book tries to show is that four broad types of revolution have occurred in modern times. Some originate in more or less popular uprisings; some are guided by ideological thinkers with a blueprint for their future utopia; others arise out of struggles for national liberation; more rarely, revolutionary change has come about as a result of coups d'ètat; or, in light of the complexity of life, often elements characteristic of all four types are in action during any given revolution.

Given the importance of revolutions over the last three centuries in shaping the modern world, it is important both to understand what happened and to look across a broad range of revolutionary events to get a grasp of their complexity. Each individual revolution is crowded with incidents and telling details, heroism and cowardice, memorable phrases and slogans whose origins are often forgotten today.

Taken together they help us to understand our own time and how it has been shaped by revolutionary upheaval. Even those societies, like Britain or America, whose revolutions took place so long ago that they have been all but forgotten, have been deeply affected by the emotions and political struggles aroused by other peoples' revolutions.

CONTAGIOUS IDEALS

Revolutions have aroused powerful reactions, ranging from sympathy to horror. Precisely because they pose fundamental questions of who should rule and why, revolutions have no natural boundaries. Specific societies may give rise to them, but as the French or Russian revolutions showed, their ideals could be attractive across their borders. International revolutionary movements could arise from the soil of a specific society. Of course, many revolutionaries expressed their creed in a universal way. The American Declaration of Independence in 1776 was a revolutionary document addressed to the world, justifying what the Americans were doing. Most revolutions since have consciously engaged in propaganda to win sympathy and support for their cause. Not all revolutions rely on human inspiration or a progressive outlook: religious ideals can have powerful socio-political consequences. From its first appearance more than fourteen hundred years ago, the message of Islam has repeatedly swept people along into what can only be called a revolutionary transformation of their way of life. Many secular revolutionaries recognised the importance of the religious model of martyrdom and faith for promoting an ideal .

YOUTHFUL REBELS

In addition to great intellectual and socio-economic factors that combine to produce a revolutionary upheaval, more intangible forces are usually at play too. For instance, the youthfulness of most revolutionaries is striking. Risk-taking, whether on the streets as a demonstrator or as dissident challenging a system despite the high chances of arrest, torture, or even death, is rarely a chance taken by the elderly, to whom life has taught the caution born of years of disappointment.

But if revolutions are rarely made by the elderly, many revolutionaries who succeed in seizing power grow old in power themselves. Sometimes revolutions are the outcome of a generational block caused by gerontocrats clinging to power and frustrating normal ambitions. Central Europe in 1848 and again in 1989 experienced revolutions that had aspects of a dramatic breaking of a logjam caused by one generation holding onto power for far too long.

Such generational revolutions are not only about frustrated ambitions, otherwise crowds would never assemble. The elderly, who block reform and reformers from power within a system, feed the deeper causes of revolution outside it. The obstinate hold on power symbolizes the regime's blocking of progress and hope.

EXTERNAL TRIGGERS

The events that actually trigger revolutionary upheaval can be external ones. War has been a major factor. Defeat in war, or the heavy burden of taxes caused by even a victorious war, can set off discontent. Defeat in war certainly was a central factor in the wave of revolutions in Russia in 1905 and even more spectacularly in 1917, or in Germany in 1918. The need to fight wars of national defence can also radicalize the situation as it did in France in 1792 when foreign invasions, intended to suppress the revolution and restore the monarchy, prompted the revolutionaries to combine terror against their opponents at home with a completely new style of revolutionary warfare. Wars of national liberation from the Dutch Revolt in the 16th century to a host of examples across the Third World in the second half of the 20th century bring with them social and economic upheaval as well as radical political changes.

Sometimes revolutionary movements trigger equally thoroughgoing reactions when one society tries to export its values to another. Outsiders can try to provoke revolution in other countries but rarely succeed unless the conditions of mass discontent already exist or unless they have overwhelming force. Che Guevara believed that only a dynamic revolutionary group could inspire widespread revolt by its own actions, but sadly for him, attempts to provoke revolution in Bolivia in 1967 led to his own humiliating capture and execution.

Stalin's Soviet Union, however, was able to expand communism into Eastern Europe after 1945 as its Red Army swept the defeated Nazi army back to Berlin. But the rise of Islamic fundamentalism in Afghanistan would have been unthinkable without the Red Army's invasion in 1979.

INTENSE DEVOTION

Just as religious reformers, like the Prophet Mohammed, had a powerful urge to spread their doctrines, so revolutionaries often have a quasi-religious faith in their cause and an almost religious zeal in promoting their ideals. Intense ideological commitment makes it easier to sacrifice oneself in what often must seem hopeless struggles. Sometimes the language of revolutionaries echoes the language of religious faith, especially in the face of apparent defeat. In 1919, shortly before she was executed, the

German revolutionary Rosa Luxemburg declared to her enemies, "Tomorrow, the revolution will raise its head again, proclaiming to your horror, 'I was, I am, I always shall be!'" In the Soviet Union, after his death in 1924, Lenin was deified and preserved in his mausoleum on Red Square in Moscow. For decades, the Soviet slogan echoed, "Lenin lives!"

FROM REVOLUTION TO TYRANNY

Revolutions in power can lose their dynamism very quickly and degenerate into tyrannies as bad as or worse than what went before. Che Guevara said, "A revolution that does not continue to grow deeper is a revolution which is retreating."

The cult of revolutions is a sign that the movements have lost their revolutionary meaning. Pierre Boulez remarked in 1989 that a "revolution worth celebrating was dead." The ossification of dynamic events in museums and mausoleums marks the failure of any particular cause.

Whether revolution itself can be said to be dead at the beginning of the 21st century remains to be seen. Complacency in the past has not been a good indicator of future outbreaks. No-one predicted the sudden collapse of Communism in 1989. I doubt if anyone will foresee the next uprising which may radically change a country, or even the world.

In the midst of the ongoing struggle in Algeria, some 27 men, women, and children were massacred on 10 February 2001 and lay draped with Algerian flags in their shantytown.

THE POWER OF
IDEOLOGY

Introduction

Ideological revolutionaries are those politicians, usually intellectuals, who have a clear vision of the future society they wish to create. The pre-conditions for any successful attempt to achieve such a blueprint are the same conditions for upheaval that any revolution requires. Deep-seated socio-economic discontent plus the discrediting of the existing system, its elite's ideas, and legitimacy are essential pre-requisites. However, what turns a revolutionary situation into an ideological transformation is that the revolution aims to achieve a new order of society that is completely and fundamentally different from the old – not simply shorn of its political, economic, or religious elite.

radical head of steam and toppled the monarchy and social hierarchy, the revolutionaries became self-conscious architects of a break with what was now a despised past and the founders of a new order. To symbolize the significance of the declaration of the French republic in September 1792, the French abandoned the Christian calendar and started to date events from Year I of their republic. (The power of this idea is reflected in its imitators, including Mussolini's fascist regime in Italy after 1922, which saw itself as reversing the Declaration of the Rights of Man of 1789 but still introduced its own fascist calendar starting from October 1922 and coming to an abrupt end in April 1945.)

CREATING A NEW ORDER

Perhaps the downfall of a regime is largely the product of impersonal and unconscious forces. France in 1789 witnessed an earth-shattering revolution that soon became a self-conscious ideological crusade for republicanism, human rights, and anti-clericalism. But in the beginning the French revolutionaries had hardly realized that what they demanded of the king was a revolution to create a new order rather than simply to return to an older imagined better state. Once the French Revolution developed its

ERASING THE PAST

The idea that history had started afresh in 1792 was a powerful symbol of the ideological urge to wipe clean the past from the minds and manners of the French people. One hundred and fifty years later, Mao Zedong in China declared that his people were "blank sheets of paper" on which he would write the "beautiful poetry" of communism. This desire to cleanse the minds of people of their pre-revolutionary (bad) habits led to the practice of brain-washing in Mao's China, but in general terms

ideological revolutions have seen repeated attempts to terrorize people into a complete and personal break with the past. This of course was always easier said than done, even for enthusiasts of the revolution. However much revolutionaries may have wanted to break with the past, they were all, in one way or another, shaped by it.

ACTS OF TERRORISM

This tragic truth underpins so much of the tendency of revolutions and revolutionaries to turn against each other as well as open opponents or vocal critics. Ideological revolutions have been pockmarked by campaigns of terror and show trials in which the non-conformity or past errors (real or

Propaganda films presented a one-sided picture of the holocaust, as in this image from Triumph of the Will, *showing storm troopers parading at Nuremberg.*

imagined) of former comrades are drowned in blood. From France in 1793–4 to Stalin's Russia in the 1930s to Khomeini's Iran after 1979, revolutions have proved to be like Saturn devouring his own children.

THE POWER OF PROPAGANDA

In spite of the fact that so many revolutions are based on a set of rigid ideals or a blueprint with a rigid goal (whether by a dead secular prophet like a Karl Marx or a living Ayatollah), it is striking how often the most rigidly ideological revolutionaries have come to power on the back of apparently pragmatic slogans and broad-based coalitions. The classic example is Lenin and the Russian communists in 1917. After three years of bloodshed in World War I, widespread food shortages made life a further misery. The communists were well aware that the mass of the Russian population were peasants with an insatiable hunger and need for more land. Lenin keenly understood these needs and offered a simple but incredibly persuasive slogan, "Peace, land, and bread" as his solution to Russia's problems. In fact, this slogan was intended to attract the masses to support a party whose real programme involved fundamental, life-altering changes.

THE FIRST IDEOLOGICAL REVOLUTION

Lenin's was the first ideological revolutionary regime that intended to transform humanity, society, and even the environment in order to create the conditions for a completely new social order: communism. As early as the 1840s, Karl Marx and Friedrich Engels anticipated the birth of communism and the disappearance of a society where hierarchy or money counted, and developed a theory of how it should happen.

Marx and Engels, like Lenin, were well aware that almost since the dawn of human society there had been a nostalgia for a lost world of human innocence and equality in some Garden of Eden. They rejected romantic, backward-looking ideas of a pre-modern socialism in favour of harnessing new technologies and methods of modern capitalist culture to produce a transformed society that did away with ownership and subordination.

To get ordinary people on board for this ambitious and ultimately flawed project, Lenin had to offer them what they wanted in the short term in order to detach the bulk of the population from his irreconcilable enemies among the reactionaries and capitalists. Lenin inverted the Biblical saying, "Those who are not for me are against me" and instead argued that in politics it was the passive majority that could prove decisive if they did not join the wrong side. For Lenin, politics was a war of minorities. It mattered that your minority was bigger and better organized than the other side. Then it would win. After victory the real work of transforming society could get under way.

INEVITABLE FAILURE

In some ways a revolution like Lenin's in Russia or Mao's in China could only end in failure since its scope was so ambitious that it could not be achieved. In that sense the Soviet attempt to create the so-called "New Man" was a project that continued until the collapse of the Soviet Union in 1991. Not only did it turn out that Soviet humanity was at heart still Russian or Latvian, but the environmental costs of Trotsky's dream of re-ordering the physical environment by "moving mountains around like so much furniture in a room" had definitely changed nature for ever, but sadly not for the better, as re-directed rivers in Central Asia dried up and dustbowls were created on steppes where collective farms were established regardless of practicality.

HOSTILITY TO REVOLUTION

Of course, it was not only dreams of human equality and a natural world ordered for mankind's common benefit that wrought havoc in the last century. Hostility to revolution spawned its own ideological fanaticisms, which in turn became counter-revolutionary dogmas of their own. It would be impossible to understand Nazi Germany and the full horror of Hitler's rule without taking into account his warped dystopian vision for the future, which fed off numerous imagined evils.

Like his mortal enemies the communists, Hitler came to power using compromise and guile, but any reading of his autobiography, *Mein Kampf,* or the vast pseudo-scientific literature of Nazi racism even before 1933, should have made clear that the Nazi leader had an ideology for a vast programme of aggression and racial re-ordering of Europe at least, and possibly the world.

The Nazis not only rejected the revolutionary heritage dating back to 1789 with its progressive and humanist ideas – admittedly more honoured in the breach than in practice – they also had no intention of defeating the left simply to let the old reactionary elites back into power. In Hitler's vocabulary, communist and reactionary were equally words of abuse. The Nazis' short period in power (1933–45) saw a whirlwind of what Hitler, in his distorted way, saw as creative destruction: whole sections of humanity were targeted for annihilation simply because they did not fit into his vision of a "healthy" racial future. Along with up to six million Jews, almost one million Gypsies, hundreds of thousands of disabled, mentally ill, and senile people and scores of thousands of homosexuals were tortured, gassed, or murdered in various ways. The urge to inflict such destruction, the will to carry it through, and the ability to find willing executioners, depended on the propagation of Hitler's extreme ideological vision.

THE COLLAPSE OF IDEOLOGICAL EMPIRES

With Hitler's defeat and death, Nazism collapsed. Other secular ideologies seemed to have lost their intellectual grip once the first generation of believers passed away. The collapse of communism in 1989 saw elderly first-generation communists, like Erich Honecker in East Germany, unable to hold back the tide of disillusionment among younger generations. Castro's survival in Cuba may well reflect his status as a charismatic living prophet of the revolution.

Ideological revolutions have often been compared to waves of religious conversions. However, early Christianity or Islam put down deeper roots than secular ideologies have so far achieved. Only time will tell whether revolutionary Islam, in Iran and elsewhere, will prove as long-lived.

The Netherlands 1585

An explosive mixture of religion, politics, and nationalism led to the Dutch revolt against Spanish overlord Philip II. Protests against the king's religious persecution and interference with the traditional way of life grew into a revolutionary war, establishing a republic in defiance of the monarchy and paving the way for religious tolerance.

explosive issue. Philip II was an intolerant Catholic for whom it was better to die a thousand deaths than rule over heretics.

Protestantism had been spreading for several decades in the Netherlands. Philip II planned to root out the religion in an inquisition similar to the infamous Spanish Inquisition. Even Catholics grew alarmed, fearing that political dissent would be

A NEW MONARCH'S INTOLERANCE

When Charles V abdicated in 1555, his son Philip II inherited the 17 provinces that made up the Netherlands. His rule extended over Spain and much of Italy and the Americas.

Completely indifferent to the traditions of the diverse territories, Philip II ran each of his lands in the same way from Spain. Claiming to provide equal justice for all, he in fact reduced the previously self-governing Dutch to the status of Spanish subjects who could neither challenge policies nor vote on taxes.

Philip II intended to raise taxes in the Netherlands to fund the Spanish troops garrisoned there. Although such taxes were unpopular, religion proved to be the

A respected landowner and natural leader, William, Prince of Orange, rallied fellow nobles, fishermen, and merchants of the coastal towns to fight for the rebel cause.

1555 *Philip II inherits the Netherlands*

5 June 1568 *Execution of Egmont and Hoorn*

January 1579 *Spain persuades Dutch Catholics to obey Philip II while seven rebel Dutch provinces continue the struggle*

1588 *Defeat of P* *II's Armada by Ang* *Dutch fleet*

1550

August 1566 *Iconoclastic fury – Protestant mobs ransack Catholic churches*

1575

November 1576 *Spanish fury – mutinous troops sack Antwerp*

10 July 1584 *Assassination of William of Orange*

26 July 1581 *Act of Abjuration – rebels denounce the right of Philip II to rule over them*

silenced as well. By the late 1560s many voiced outrage at the tax burden and at royal representatives who overrode local assemblies in order to centralize authority.

CATHOLICS AND PROTESTANTS UNITE

In the face of heavy-handed government and religious persecution, Catholics and Protestants alike agreed on the need to keep their traditional liberties and avoid being ruled on the Spanish model.

When riots broke out in 1566, fury led Protestants to smash Catholic symbols deemed idolatrous. In response Philip II flooded the Netherlands with Spanish troops in 1567. Their commander, the Duke of Alva, threatened to make a New World out of the Netherlands, alluding to the merciless massacre of the Indians of Mexico and Peru by Spanish conquistadors.

PERSECUTION INSPIRES A REBELLION

Alva executed aristocratic critics, such as counts Egmont and Hoorn in 1568, to frighten the the rest of the population into acquiescence. Instead, rebellion rose with William, Prince of Orange, at its helm.

Though rebellion seemed futile in the face of the Spanish army, the coastal Dutch had one advantage: they could use the North Sea as a supply route and way of attacking and retreating with impunity. In 1572 exiled Protestant Dutch rebels captured the port of Brill. Using the network of canals and dykes that kept the sea from swamping low-lying country, they flooded large stretches of land to beat back the Spanish.

A DEFIANT NEW REPUBLIC

Although at first insisting on their loyalty to the king, the rebels eventually renounced allegiance to Philip II and proclaimed that rulers existed to serve their subjects not the other way round. Reduced to seven defiant provinces, they formed a republic. Philip II would pour all the resources of his empire into trying to reverse this bold decision.

With English and French aid to the Dutch, the war spread around the globe as rebel privateers raided Philip's vast Latin American empire. Profits from piracy and growing worldwide trade helped fund the long Dutch struggle with Spain. Catastrophic defeats, such as that of the Spanish Armada in 1588, weakened Spain's position. After a truce and then renewed war, a bankrupt Spain recognized the Dutch Republic in 1648.

The Dutch Republic, rich in commerce and predominantly Protestant (tolerating Catholics and welcoming Jewish refugees from Spain), was a model of successful self-government, even influencing nearby England.

1621 War resumes

1600

1609 Truce between Spain and the Dutch rebels

1625

5 April 1648 Treaty of Westphalia: Spain finally accepts Dutch independence

1650

England 1642–9

The trial and execution of King Charles I in January 1649 marked the climax of an unprecedented revolution. Though kings had been overthrown and killed before, never had one been put on trial and executed by his subjects, who then proclaimed a republic.

Throughout the 1630s, the English king had ruled without calling Parliament. Although Parliament did not meet at set intervals, over the previous century Englishmen had come to expect regular sessions. Interest groups in the country – such as landed gentry or merchants of important cities – provided the bulk of the elected members of the House of Commons, while the House of Lords consisted of the greatest landowners, bishops of the Church of England, and favoured courtiers of the king. Wise kings ruled with the consent of the majority of these groups, taking into account their economic, political, and religious views.

Since Henry VIII broke with the Catholic Church by Act of Parliament in 1534, England's Catholic minority was small and unpopular. Most Englishmen associated Protestantism with political liberty, relying on a system of government in which the king consulted their representatives in Parliament before making great changes or raising taxes.

After the death of the childless Queen Elizabeth I in 1603, the English Crown passed to her cousin, James VI of Scotland. The new monarch, while insensitive to English traditions, lacked the energy and single-mindedness to provoke much trouble. However, his son, Charles I, who succeeded him in 1625, was a very different character.

THE ELEVEN YEARS' TYRANNY

Charles I shared his father's high view of the rights of monarchs but imitated the absolutist methods of his European contemporaries. Quarrels with the House of Commons over taxes to fund disastrous foreign wars soon led MPs to attack the king's abuse of his executive powers. The crisis climaxed in 1629 when the House of Commons defied the king's order to dissolve, while passing resolutions condemning arbitrary royal acts and asserting his subjects' rights. Charles I forced Parliament's dissolution, imprisoned three ex-MPs without trial, and ruled without consulting his subjects again.

Although the king eventually abandoned wars against France and Spain, he still needed money to fund his government and court. So

1625 Charles I succeeds his father, James I

1639–40 Charles I's war against the Scots

1641 Long Parliament opens – finally dissolved in 1660

1648 Pride's Purge of the English Parliament

20–27 January 1649 Trial of Charles I

16 December 1653 Oliver Cromwell proclaimed Lord Protector

1625

1629–1640 The Eleven Years' Tyranny – Charles I rules without Parliament

August 1642 Civil War starts

1646 Charles I surrenders to Scots

1645 Charles I defeated at Battle of Naseby

1650

30 January 1649 Execution of Charles I

3 September 1658 Death of Oliver Cromwell

between 1629 and 1640 Charles I revived half-forgotten feudal levies and extended local taxes to fund England's coastal defence.

The king compounded his unpopularity in the 1630s by only appointing bishops whose theology and style of worship seemed alarmingly Catholic. Their emphasis on what the Archbishop of Canterbury, William Laud, called "the beauty of holiness" appealed to the king's aesthetic side. Puritan country landowners, however, found this subversive to the English Protestant way of life.

In 1637 Charles I started to impose the same religious views on the Scots, whose Protestant roots were deep, but they promptly rebelled. Unsuppressed by his poorly funded army, the Scots occupied northern England in 1639.

In 1640, Charles I called Parliament for the first time since 1629 to obtain their support to fight Scotland. His appeals failed. After 11 years of tyranny, Parliament resolved to pass laws preventing the abuse of their traditional rights and any weakening of Protestantism.

One by one Charles I's key ministers were picked off by Parliamentary pressure. In May 1641 an Act of Parliament ordered execution of the king's minister, the Earl of Strafford, allegedly for plotting to bring an Irish Catholic army to suppress Parliament and Protestantism. Charles I signed the death sentence to save his family from the London mob demanding Strafford's head.

KING'S POWER LIMITED

Although Charles I capitulated on a host of Parliament's demands, his obvious reluctance heightened suspicions about him. Then in 1641, Irish Catholics rebelled against Protestant minority rule. Reports of massacres in Ireland and rumours that the king would use the Irish Catholic army to suppress Protestantism, radicalized the popular mood. In turn, radicals in the House of Commons proposed to remove the king's right to command the army, while also effectively abolishing the royal prerogative, special courts, and the bishops of the Church of England. They obliged the king to agree to regular Parliaments, at least every three years. Reducing the king to a figurehead without any real executive power went too far for conservative MPs. In their eyes, rabble-rousing radical MPs threatened to overturn the social order.

Detecting this shift in mood in January 1642, Charles I struck back. With an armed posse he stormed the House of Commons to arrest five MPs he regarded as the ringleaders of opposition. In response to this unprecedented entrance, the Speaker refused to answer when asked where they went. Though humiliated, Charles I left and rallied support from nobles and gentry who feared a collapse of the monarchy and a social revolution in which tenants poached

29 May 1660
*Restoration of monarchy
– Charles II returns
from exile*

November 1688
*William of Orange
invades and James II
flees to France*

*1707 Act of Union unites
England and Scotland under
the Westminster Parliament*

1675

*1685 Charles II
succeeded by James II*

February 1689 *Bill of Rights
and William and Mary
proclaimed joint sovereigns*

1700

*1701 Act of Settlement –
Parliament decides who will
inherit the throne*

game and refused to pay rents. Parliamentary leaders used the king's actions and allegations about his French Catholic queen's plotting to muster support on their side.

CIVIL WAR

In the summer of 1642, skirmishing led to open warfare. Once civil war began, Parliament clearly had most of the strategic advantages. Charles I relied on cavalry drawn from loyal nobility and gentry but had limited economic resources. Mercantile wealth was a key ingredient to military success and Parliament's dependence on the resources of cities like London, strengthened the influence of its leading citizens on Parliament, tilting the balance of power away from landowners.

Nevertheless, at first, both sides struggled to organize armies after 150 years of internal peace. Neither the long-haired royal cavaliers nor the short-cropped puritan roundheads could achieve decisive victories. But Parliament recognized the need for professional forces to replace ill-disciplined local volunteers and levies. A New Model Army was organized in 1644, led by Sir Thomas Fairfax and Oliver Cromwell. Drawn from a wide spectrum of puritanical Englishmen, this was the first revolutionary army with a clear ideology. Cromwell himself made belief not social origins the basis for promotion, replying to a colleague's fear that his officers were unsuitable men: "I had rather have a plain russet-coated captain that knows what he fights for...than that which you call a gentleman and is nothing else." The war shifted decisively in 1644 when the New Model Army routed the royalists in the north of England at Marston Moor near York.

In 1645, Charles I's armies were finally defeated at Naseby and his temporary capital, Oxford, capitulated in 1646. The king surrendered to the Scots, hoping to conspire with them against the English, but was turned over to Parliament in return for a promise that England would adopt Scottish-style Protestantism – and a large cash grant.

A DIVIDED PARLIAMENT IS PURGED

Holding Charles I prisoner posed a dilemma for Parliament and began to divide the MPs. Some wanted to deal with him as their rightful king but to impose strict conditions on future behaviour. But could he be trusted? Conservative Parliamentary leader, the Earl of Manchester, summed up the problem, "If we beat the king 99 times, he remains king, but if he defeats us once, we shall all hang." For two years Parliament tried to hammer out a compromise whereby the king would guarantee Parliament, Protestantism, and property rights. But Charles I showed he could not be trusted when conspiring royalists in England and Scotland started a second civil war in 1648.

Cromwell's troops quickly routed the royalists and denounced the king as "Charles Stuart, that man of blood". Cromwell led Parliament to put Charles I on trial for treason against his subjects. This step was too radical for many Parliamentarians. So, to safeguard their plan, Cromwell and the radicals sent troops in December 1648 to purge the House of Commons of moderate opponents of the king.

At his trial and execution, Charles I behaved with remarkable courage and dignity. By arguing that if the army could purge Parliament and put their king on trial, no one was safe from arbitrary action by Cromwell and his colleagues, the king skilfully turned the arguments of his critics on their head: "If a power without law may make laws... I do not know what subject can be sure of his life, or anything that he calls his own." Charles I's behaviour at the trial and fearless acceptance of his fate on the

The king's trial shocked conservatives and his execution outside Whitehall on 30 January 1649 fuelled doubts and fears about the power of the new republic.

executioner's block helped sow seeds of doubt among the propertied classes – many of whom already worried about the rise to power of low-born men, such as the ex-brewer's drayman, Colonel Thomas Pride.

CROMWELL STAMPS OUT RADICALS

With the king dead and bishops abolished, the House of Lords was next to go. The new English republic was ruled by the House of Commons alone, a reduction to an 80-strong Rump of the old 558-strong house. The new regime claimed to rule in the name of the people, but refused any challenges to it.

Soon an even more radical group threatened the regime by challenging the class system – with their aim to "level"

society by demanding radical equality in voting rights for every citizen under the law. The so-called Levellers wanted to extend political participation beyond the narrow confines represented by the Rump. Alarmed at this threat to his power base, and intolerant of anyone more radical than himself, Cromwell rounded up and shot key Leveller agitators in the summer of 1649.

AN UNSUSTAINABLE REPUBLIC

Although the republican army could defeat all rivals and conquered Scotland and Ireland

in wars, politicians proved unable to bring about the puritanical kingdom of heaven on earth desired by men such as Cromwell. Corruption inside the Rump led Cromwell to stage a coup in 1653 to purge it once and for all. He summoned a hand-picked Parliament of Saints, but the quarrelsome fundamentalists proved less able to govern than the Rump.

With a show of reluctance, Cromwell assumed supreme power with the title of Lord Protector at the end of 1653. A revolution challenging a king's attempt to rule without consulting his subjects led to rule by one man. To be fair, Cromwell was uncomfortable with his position. He tried to revive Parliament and even created a new house of lords, the Other House, to create a constitutional basis for his regime. In effect his experiments led to the restoration of the monarchy. With Cromwell's death the English republic began to disintegrate. Though his son, Richard, was accepted as successor and Lord Protector, he lacked his father's political charisma and skills. Politicians in London soon decided to negotiate with the exiled Charles II.

Though Charles II returned in May 1660, the landscape of the monarchy had changed forever. Old Parliamentarians, such as General Monk or others who had done well out of the Republic, wanted to protect their gains. Meanwhile the English elite wanted a compromise on political power, religion, and property rights, which Charles I had failed to

The commanding Oliver Cromwell, landowner and MP, shaped the fledgling republic first as leader of the New Model Army and later as Lord Protector after 1653.

make in the 1640s. Though Charles II intrigued to hold onto the powers left to him, he wisely turned a deaf ear to royalist exiles wanting a return to the 1630s. A few token regicides were persecuted for voting for Charles I's death, but the majority of Parliament transitioned smoothly from serving the republic to serving the restored and tempered monarchy.

PROTESTANT ENGLAND THREATENED

Charles II's relaxed style and political shrewdness managed to calm repeated threats of political crisis. But after his death in 1685, his brother, James II, a Catholic who lacked all of his skills, succeeded. To most Englishmen, Catholicism equalled despotism and James II did little to disabuse them of the notion. He flouted the laws banning English Catholics from holding public office, especially in the army. His interference with the courts and his alliance with Catholic France alarmed English Protestants.

Already elderly in 1685, James II might have been tolerated by the English elite if the heir to the throne had remained his Protestant daughter, Mary, who was married to the Dutch Prince, William of Orange. However, in June 1688, James II's wife gave birth to a son, who was bound to be raised Catholic and carry on his father's arbitrary policies. The threat to English Protestants was so obvious that even the bishops of the restored Church of England joined in a plot to bring William of Orange from Holland to force James II to back down.

THE GLORIOUS REVOLUTION

When William of Orange invaded in November 1688, Protestant soldiers deserted and the nobles pressured James II on their demands. Fearing for his life, James II fled to France, making way for his daughter, Mary, and her husband, William of Orange, to become joint monarchs in February 1689.

William and Mary had to accept a Bill of Rights limiting the powers of the state over its subjects, and agree to Parliaments every three years, although it met annually to pass the budget and renew the Mutiny Act giving the king authority over the army. In 1701, Parliament even determined the future succession to the throne by passing the Act of Settlement, excluding any Catholic successors of James II.

What became known as the Glorious Revolution of 1688 turned England into a state dominated by Parliament. England absorbed Scotland (in 1707) and Ireland (1801) into this new political system and the monarch gradually lost all political power, becoming a mere symbol of the country. The events of 1688 led to a revolutionary transfer of power from king to the classes represented in Parliament, with laws and taxes decided according to their interests and wishes. This new all-powerful Parliament claimed sovereignty over Britain and her growing colonial possessions in the 18th century. To the restive colonists in North America two generations later, the absolute sovereignty of the British Parliament seemed just as oppressive as arbitrary rule by a king.

America 1776

The influence of the American Revolution in the 1770s is still felt today, more than 225 years later. What started as an old-fashioned tax revolt against the British colonial authorities in North America soon developed into a war of national liberation – the first revolution to make universal claims. The rebels' Declaration of Independence asserted, "We hold these truths to be self-evident, that all men are created equal", and echoed down the centuries, inspiring revolutions around the world.

TAXES AND TRADE RESTRICTIONS

Although many of the colonies' early settlers had fled England to practise their faith free from royal scrutiny, they realized that without protection from British troops their largely self-governing colonies might fall under the control of Catholic France, which then ruled Canada and much of the vast territory to their west. By 1763 Britain defeated France in the Seven Years' War and then annexed Canada, alleviating the Americans' fear. But afterwards, heavily indebted by the costs of the war, the British Parliament levied new taxes on the colonies to pay for their share of the continuing

British garrison based there. Americans resented these new taxes, both because they seemed unnecessary with the defeat of France and because they were not consulted. The British Parliament, though proud of its heritage of 17th-century revolutions against kings who tried to tax at home without consent, proved incapable of understanding that the Americans saw themselves as victims of a similarly arbitrary imposition of taxes.

The Stamp Act of 1765 subjected many business transactions to new duties. Worse still, the British refused to allow the colonists to trade directly with other European countries. Only goods carried by British registered ships could be exported or imported. Having developed extensive trading links with Europe and other parts of the Americas, traders deeply resented this attempt by British merchants to monopolize American trade.

GROWING DISCONTENT

The 13 colonies boasted 2.5 million inhabitants and the second biggest English-speaking city in the world (Philadelphia, by 1770). British taxes and trade restrictions impacted affluent and politically aware

1763 *Britain's victory in Seven Years' War eliminates French threat to 13 British colonies in North America*

12 March 1770 *Boston Massacre*

16 December 1773 *Boston Tea Party*

1765

1770

1775

1765 *The Stamp Act*

April 1775 *War breaks out between British forces and colonists*

4 July 17
Declarati
Independ
signed

people, not primitive colonists on the edge of the known world. Lawyers and intellectuals, like young John Adams of Massachusetts and Benjamin Franklin, whose scientific theories and enlightened ideas found an audience in Europe, developed political arguments undercutting British claims to power over the colonies.

Denied their rights, the Americans grew more radical and discontented. In 1770 protests about new duties on tea and the general downturn in trade led to a bloody confrontation in Boston between local demonstrators and the British garrison, leaving five Americans dead. This Boston Massacre marked the first bloodshed between Americans and British troops. In December 1773 some Bostonians, disguised as Indians, engaged in a symbolic prank by climbing aboard British ships in the harbour and dumping chests of high-duty tea into the water. This Boston Tea Party provoked the British Parliament to punish the city by closing its port, which antagonized many more Americans. Nevertheless parliament continued to create legislation for the colonies into the 1770s, deaf to the increasingly popular slogan, "No taxation without representation."

AMERICA'S FIRST CONGRESS

Denied representation in the distant London Parliament, local colonial assemblies formed their own representative body in North America in defiance of Britain and, in September 1774, met together for the first time as a Continental Congress to discuss

This cartoon from The Broadside, *at the time of the Boston Massacre, criticizes British policies against the colonies, portrayed as killing the goose that laid the golden eggs.*

19 October 1781 *Battle of Yorktown – decisive British defeat*

17 September 1787 *US constitution adopted by constitutional convention*

1780

1783 *Treaty of Versailles – Britain recognizes American independence*

1785

1789 *George Washington becomes first President of the United States*

1790

their grievances. They agreed to boycott British goods as retaliation against measures imposed on them. Protests and riots reflected the growing divide with Britain and on 19 April 1775 troops clashed at Lexington outside Boston, Massachusetts. Although the British garrison in Boston hoped to seize the local militia's arsenal, American irregulars forced them to retreat, using guerrilla tactics. Soon the British army was besieged by the embryonic Continental Army.

Once war broke out, there was no turning back for the rebels. One leader, Patrick Henry, declared, "Give me liberty or give me death." The Continental Congress agreed to the Declaration of Independence drafted by Thomas Jefferson on 4 July 1776, which finalized the divorce with Great Britain. It set out both the new American theory of the

Washington's crossing of the Delaware River in December 1776 preceded his surprise attack on the British at the Battle of Trenton the next day, turning the tide of the war.

inalienable right to self-government and a long list of grievances against the British. The Declaration of Independence inspired an outburst of iconoclasm and symbols of British rule were toppled and torn down. Although united in their defiance of British rule, it took 11 years for the new United States to adopt a constitution and form a federal state in 1787.

THE COLONIES UNITE FOR WAR

In spite of uncertainty about the nature of their union, in 1776 the separate states that made up colonies began to coordinate a war effort against Britain while Britain in turn sent a field army to suppress the rebellion. The wisdom of Benjamin Franklin's observation, "Be assured if we don't all hang together, we shall certainly hang separately", encouraged even the most narrow-minded rebels to recognize that each of the colonies had to cooperate in order to avoid re-conquest by Britain. The Virginian, George Washington, who served in the war against France, was appointed commander-in-chief.

WAR ON THE FRONTIER

The British government presumed that its regular forces would soon crush the rebels. Although British forces had conventional superiority, they faced a new type of war. Rebel leader Alexander Hamilton urged the American forces to avoid set-piece battles that British troops were trained for and instead to harass and exhaust them by frequent skirmishes. As early as 1775 in Lexington, the Americans alarmed the British by refusing to fight conventionally in straight lines across the battlefield, preferring to shoot from behind trees and other un-gentlemanly places. With their frontier tradition, the Americans used hit-and-run tactics to disrupt British supplies, forcing them to devote too many men to garrison duty. The war was unpopular in Britain where leading politicians argued for listening to the Americans' demands and trying to compromise with them. Unable to recruit enough British men willing to fight in America, George III's government paid 40,000 mercenaries from places like the German state of Hesse, to garrison North America. This enraged the Americans and strengthened their resistance.

Trying to fight a distant war made planning and coordinating strategy very difficult. When the British tried to split the colonies by sending an army down from Canada to cut them in two, Americans harried them on an exhausting march through the backwoods on the eastern edge of the colonies. At Saratoga in October 1777, the British were finally surrounded and forced to surrender.

Saratoga changed the situation radically in America and abroad. For the first time, Americans had defeated a British army in battle. The harsh conditions of the winter of 1776–7, when Washington's army was reduced to a huddled few thousand men in rags, gave way to optimism and rallied more Americans to their new star-spangled banner. As in other revolutions and wars of liberation, rivals of the embattled Britain seized the opportunity to avenge past defeats. Long-term opponents, France and Spain, joined the fray, though failed to recognize the risk of American ideology infecting their own colonies.

The widening of the war drew off British resources to other areas of combat, but it also encouraged their generals to adopt a riskier strategy in the hope of knocking out the Americans before too much French help arrived. British forces tried to destroy the resistance by launching a sweeping campaign through the southern colonies in 1780–1, but local loyalist forces couldn't hold ground against Washington's troops without British back-up. As early as 1776, the British commander-in-chief, Henry Clinton, admitted, "There does not now exist in America a number of friends of the [British] government sufficient to defend themselves when the troops are withdrawn." Britain lacked the forces to hold the territory and London could not afford to send more troops 3,000 miles across the Atlantic while war with neighbouring France intensified.

THE SCALES ARE TIPPED

Without French assistance, particularly at sea, the war might have dragged on for years. French volunteers like the Marquis de Lafayette, who embraced American revolutionary ideas and later played a major role in the French Revolution, helped Washington's forces but the arrival of regular French troops and supplies increasingly tipped the balance against the British even in formal battles. The French navy, rebuilt at vast expense since 1763, also played a major role by blockading the British forces in North America and drawing British resources south to defend Britain's West Indian colonies.

The combination of Washington's army and the French navy brought decisive British defeat at Yorktown on the Virginia coast in October 1781. The British commander, Lord Cornwallis, found his British field army trapped between the Americans on land and the French at sea and was forced to agree to a humiliating surrender, during which a band played The World Turned Upside Down.

INDEPENDENCE AT LAST

Unable to replace the defeated field army, eventually British rule collapsed in those parts still garrisoned by British troops. Lord North, the Prime Minister, admitted, "It is all over." Peace and recognition of American independence came in 1783.

With ties to Britain severed, remaining Americans who had supported Britain were seen as traitors. After 1783 over 100,000 fled to Canada or back to Britain. A few lynchings and much plundering encouraged them on their way. Compared with later revolutions, however, the American Revolution saw remarkably little bloodletting. This reflected how the revolutionaries saw themselves as inheritors of the British rule of law tradition, which the British Parliament arbitrarily denied them. The American Revolution against British rule was based on the principles and rights that the British claimed for themselves in 1688. The ideologists of the revolution, like Thomas Jefferson and Benjamin Franklin, had crafted those claims into universal rights. This chimed in with Enlightenment thinking in Europe where the claims of tradition and hereditary right were increasingly challenged in intellectual circles.

THE IMPACT OF AMERICAN IDEAS

French success in the American war proved a pyrrhic victory for her young King Louis XVI. Not only did radical American ideas about liberty and democracy return with French soldiers like Lafayette, but the cost of the war sent the royal debt spiralling out of control, causing a financial crisis in France and events that led to the collapse of its absolute monarchy in 1789.

Spain's vast Latin American empire was also shaken by the effects of the war. Envious recognition that the North Americans had determined their own fate and cut rigid ties to a distant European capital inspired Spanish colonies to do the same.

American ideas about limited government powers and the federalism enshrined in the Constitution offered a model of political democracy with enormous influence into our own time. Its emphasis on individual

Hemmed in by French naval forces and harried by the Continental Army, General Cornwallis with nearly 8,000 British soldiers surrendered in Yorktown, 19 October 1781.

rights and limitations on the powers of government were completely new. Subsequent revolutions and political reforms led others to draft constitutions, in imitation of the rights and mechanics of government enshrined in the US constitution, but none has proved as long-lasting. The Constitution's division of political power between the elected executive President and the law-making Congress with the Supreme Court as a watchdog over both, and over the governments of the individual states that make up the United States, turned out to be the most resilient written constitution in history, one which could survive civil war in the 1860s and more recent social and economic upheavals.

France 1789

The storming of the Bastille, the prison-fortress in Paris, on 14 July 1789, is one of the enduring images of revolution – a telling picture of a people's uprising that toppled one of the world's most powerful and repressive monarchies. With idealism and violence at its heart, the French Revolution, even more than America's War of Independence, became a template for understanding future revolutions.

A BANKRUPT MONARCHY

In 1774, the youthful Louis XVI came to the throne ill equipped for the task. Although conscientious and well intentioned, he failed to grasp the problems facing the monarchy and French society. His Austrian queen, Marie Antoinette, presided over court nobility whose lavish lives were gossiped about and criticized by the excluded and oppressed masses. The queen's excesses were widely blamed for France's debts. The cost of aiding American independence in 1783 and France's subsequent rearmament only increased the monarchy's financial woes.

Unlike the British government, the French king had no effective way of raising revenue from the lucrative sources in France. His

ancestors had agreed to relieve both the landed nobility and the Catholic Church of direct taxation in return for their loyalty and acceptance of royal absolute power. Direct taxes fell upon the poorest, who had to pay the onerous poll tax (the *taille*). By the late 1780s, tax revenue hardly covered the interest on royal debts.

A CONSTITUTIONAL CHALLENGE

Bankruptcy drove Louis XVI and his advisers to acknowledge that the king alone could not solve France's problems. For the first time since 1614, the king summoned representatives of his subjects to an Estates-General – a gathering of the clergy, nobility and common people (the Third Estate) – in May 1789. He expected that all would dutifully agree to new taxes and the reduction of elite privileges. However, the representatives of the Third Estate, joined by progressive nobles and a few clerics, challenged the whole way France had been governed for two centuries.

When the king refused to listen to radical demands that the three Estates sit together as one house in which the Third Estate would predominate, and ordered the

14 July 1789 *Storming of the Bastille*

4 May 1789 *Estates-General meet*

20 June 1789 *Tennis Court Oath: The Estates-General defies Louis XVI and declares itself the National Assembly*

26 December 1790 *National Assembly abolishes Pope's authority in France*

1790

6 October 1789 *A mob led by the women of Paris I forces Louis XVI to leave Versailles*

4 August 1789 *National Assembly abolishes feudalism*

27 June 1791 *Royal family's flight to Varennes and capture*

21 September 1792 *Republic proclaimed*

10 August 1792 *Tuileries stormed by Paris mob and monarchy suspended*

23 January 1793 *Trial and execution of Louis XVI*

6 April 1793 *Committee of Public Safety established*

16 October 1793 *Execu of Marie Antoinette*

17 September 1793 *Law of Suspects extends Terror*

This broadsheet dramatically depicts the storming of the Bastille on 14 July 1789 when a blood-thirsty mob of over 300 besieged the fortress, outraged by overwhelming taxes.

dissolution of the Estates in June 1789, the representatives openly defied him and declared themselves the National Assembly, representing all the people of France.

This constitutional challenge was compounded by the social upheaval gathering momentum across France. The 1780s had seen the French population boom while bad weather and old-fashioned agricultural practices contributed to food shortages and inflation, threatening the survival of millions of the poor.

DRAMATIC REFORMS

The stand-off between the king and the National Assembly climaxed with the events of 14 July. Rumours that the king was going to dissolve the Assembly and repudiate his debts and public outrage at the alleged hoarding of food by royal officials, who

pril 1794 *Execution of the great
or, Georges Danton, and other
evolutionary leaders*

October 1795 *Directory of five
established to rule French Republic*

9 November 1799 *Napoleon
Bonaparte's coup d'état –
proclaims the end
of the revolution*

1804 *Napoleon crowns himself
"Emperor of the French"*

1815 *Napoleon's final
defeat at Waterloo and
return of French monarchy
with foreign troops*

795

1800

—8 July 1794 *Thermidor coup
ainst Robespierre*

profited from re-selling the food at high prices, incited revolt on the streets of Paris. Instead of suppressing the crowds, royal troops joined them. In revolts around France, soldiers refused to defend the authorities.

Louis XVI at last capitulated to the National Assembly's demands and dramatic reforms abolished the centuries-old class distinctions between nobles and common people. At the end of August 1789, the Declaration of the Rights of Man proclaimed "men are born free and equal in their rights" and repudiated traditional theories of the divine right of kings to rule by declaring "the fundamental source of all sovereignty resides in the nation." In the future the citizens of France would decide on the laws that governed them.

The Declaration of the Rights of Man summed up the enlightened thinking of the 18th century with its criticism of hereditary distinctions and divine sanction for them. The privileges of kings, nobles and bishops were supposed to be replaced by equality before the law and equal rights. The revolutionary slogan "Liberty, Equality, Fraternity" seemed about to be put into practice, but the pressures that sparked the revolution were hardly exhausted.

VIOLENCE SWEEPS FRANCE

Although Parisians had been key in toppling the central government machinery and forcing Louis XVI to make concession after concession, France was of course still a largely rural society. Across the provinces, peasants revolted against their feudal lords. This widespread disorder shattered the old regime and pushed the members of the National Assembly, many of them from the old privileged classes, to try to calm the situation on 4 August 1789 by proclaiming the destruction "in its entirety of the feudal regime." However, peasants who had anticipated freedom from all the dues and restrictions imposed on them by the nobility were angered to learn that the National Assembly expected them to pay for the privilege of abolishing many of these feudal rights. This disappointment radicalized many in the countryside and weakened what remained of royal authority. Peasants ransacked their lords' country manors, destroying records of rents and feudal obligations.

Abiding resentment of old privileges, fears about the food supply, and suspicions about the king's sincerity in accepting the revolution meant that the legal reforms passed by the National Assembly did not calm the popular mood, especially in Paris. In October 1789, Louis XVI faced further humiliation when a great crowd led by poor women marched to Versailles and forced the royal family to come back with them to Paris as prisoners. Lafayette, commander of the new National Guard (formed to protect the revolution from backlash), saved the king from violence. But the influence of moderates, like Lafayette, who looked to the American political model, was waning as more radical forces emerged with the collapse of royal power.

A REPUBLIC IS BORN

Louis XVI's brothers and many nobles fled abroad looking for help from fellow monarchs. Fear of these émigrés combined with continuing economic hardships pushed the revolution into a cycle of growing violence. Louis XVI's attempt to flee France in June 1791 confirmed radicals in their distrust of him. The invasion of France in 1792, by Prussian and Austrian troops determined to restore Louis XVI's full power, condemned the monarchy and the royal family. Unintimidated by the invaders, Parisians stormed Louis XVI's palace of the Tuileries, massacred the king's remaining guards and servants and took the royal family prisoner.

A republic was proclaimed. To symbolize a complete break with the past, a new calendar was adopted to replace the old Christian one, the names of days and months were changed and a 10-day week was introduced along with the decimal system. The republicans regarded the Catholic Church as a bastion of the old order and by 1794 were trying to suppress it. Titles were abolished and everyone became simply "Citizen."

AN AGE OF MASS WARFARE

The new republic was born in savage circumstances in September 1792 when royalist suspects were massacred as the Prussian army approached Paris. Foreign invasion provoked a wave of nationalism.

Against the professional Prussian troops the new republic summoned a *levée en masse* in which all Frenchmen could be conscripted to defend the revolution. Led by a core of ex-royal officers and inspired by revolutionary idealism, this new mass army swept away the Prussians, using daring new tactics on the battlefield. Instead of wars between professional mercenary armies, the French launched an age of mass warfare. As the new regime battled with foreign enemies and economic upheaval, tensions swelled in Paris, fuelling fears of sabotage from sympathizers with the monarchy. The terror reached a feverish pitch and the ex-king fell as its first victim. The radical republicans intended the trial and execution of Louis XVI as a decisive break with the past. (It was also a reversal of their abolition of the death penalty, once a symbol of the old regime's cruelty.)

COUNTER–REVOLUTIONARY BACKLASH

The republicans thought that with the ex-king dead, counter-revolution would collapse. But criticism of the new regime persisted. In the countryside, especially in the south and west, open rebellion stirred. Many ordinary people resented the burdens of conscription, war taxation and the anti-religious trend of the Parisian revolutionaries. Rural opposition to the rebellion, combined with rumours of counter-revolutionary plotters in league with the émigrés abroad, fuelled a savage determination to stamp out opposition. The mass panic grew worse as civil war compounded problems like food shortages.

Rather than quelling the counter-revolution, the show trial of Citizen Louis Capet (to give the king his family name) in January 1793 and the trial and execution of his widow, Marie Antoinette, acted as a stepping stone to a wider reign of terror and paranoia. Soon the persecution of real and imagined enemies of the revolution spread like wildfire.

THE REIGN OF TERROR

LA POULLE D'AUTRÿCHE,

This illustration and its caption play on the similarly spelled French words for Austrian and ostrich, a not too subtle reference to Marie Antoinette and her love of finery.

In a reign that came to be known as "the Terror", institutions such as the Committee of Public Safety established a ruthless and arbitrary regime. It was justified by an appeal to a simple "us-versus-them" mentality. Robespierre insisted that "The People are the sole Sovereign" in May 1793, dividing the population of France into "the People and its enemies". Revolutionary laws provided no rights to those suspected of opposing the People. Tribunals regarded "lack of enthusiasm" for the revolution as proof of guilt, so almost anyone who hadn't taken part in demonstrations of support for the new authorities could face trial. Ordinary citizens settled scores by informing on neighbours for being "aristocrats," a term which now came to mean anyone suspected of opposing the revolution.

A revolutionary tribunal was established to provide summary justice. In June 1794, it was proclaimed that "The penalty for all offences within the jurisdiction of the Revolutionary Tribunal is death." About 30,000 French people were denounced as "enemies of the people" and guillotined between the years of 1793–4. Most were ordinary people who fell foul of informers in the atmosphere of suspicion generated by foreign invasion, food shortages and rumours of plots. The Terror was supposed to intimidate reactionaries into obedience but in practice it terrorized supporters of the republic as well. The revolution was devouring itself.

The very radicalization of the Terror was undermining Robespierre and his colleagues. Revolutionaries feared for their own safety and Parisian crowds, demoralized by hyperinflation and shortages, no longer followed where the radicals led. A group within the republican regime decided to forestall any charges against them by staging a pre-emptive coup against Robespierre at the end of July 1794. Along with his brother and other key "terrorists," Robespierre was hustled, on the 10th day of the month known as Thermidor, to the guillotine. Thermidor came to symbolize the moment in revolutions when the radicals are toppled by their more moderate comrades and the drive for revolutionary perfection is tempered by pragmatic politics. The émigrés hopes that Robespierre's fall would produce a reaction in favour of monarchy were soon dashed. The Republic stabilized under the rule of a five-man Directory from 1795.

Although the exiled royalists hoped that the bloodletting of Thermidor 1794 was a prelude to a restoration of the monarchy, France's new rulers proved determined to maintain the republic. They took harsh measures against counter-revolutionaries and continued the war abroad.

THE RISE IN NATIONALISM

The French Declaration of the Rights of Man was seen as subversive and threatening by monarchs across Europe and provoked foreign intervention in 1792. After repelling the invaders, the French troops swarmed eastwards across the Rhine, spreading revolutionary ideas and abolishing the feudal regime as they advanced. New republics sprang up in the Netherlands and Switzerland and as far south as Naples in imitation of France.

But for all the French rhetoric about the rights of man and universal brotherhood, the war promoted a new and surprising reactionary phenomenon – nationalism. At first French nationalism was defensive and sprang up while the country resisted invasion, but with victory came an ugly turn. France's military success was taken as proof of French superiority and over the next 20 years French conquests provoked nationalist uprisings in Spain and Germany and helped to feed the spread of mutually exclusive and hostile nationalisms across Europe throughout the 19th century.

War promoted the political influence of successful generals. None knew better how to turn military glory into political power than the 30-year-old Corsican, Napoleon Bonaparte. In November 1799, he staged the first coup d'état, seizing control of France, which was wearied by years of warfare, inflation, and shortages. At first, most French people accepted the new authoritarian ruler who satisfied many reactionaries by declaring the revolution "is ended" after 10 years of upheaval, while also reassuring many radicals by refusing to reverse the revolution's many social and legal changes. It took the self-proclaimed emperor's complete military defeat in 1815 to restore the monarchy. Even so, when the new King Louis XVIII returned after Waterloo, he had to accept that the revolution of 14 July 1789 had changed the political landscape forever. Repeated upheavals in 1830, 1848, and 1871 proved that the ideals of 1789 and social turmoil in France were far from exhausted.

The Effects of 1789

The impact of the French Revolution was felt far beyond the European states bordering the new French republic in the 1790s. French revolutionary ideals were spread throughout much of Europe by her armies as well as by sympathizers. Famously the 1960s Chinese communist revolutionary, Chou En-lai, replied when asked what he thought the impact of the French Revolution had been on world history, "It is too early to say"!

Already in the 1790s, aftershocks of the radical developments in France rippled across the Atlantic. French ideas of popular sovereignty and the effect of the revolutionary wars in cutting off Spain's Latin American colonies from the motherland, which was occupied by Napoleon in 1808, meant that aspirations for independence took wing from Mexico in the north, travelling to Argentina and Chile in the south.

The most charismatic figure in the Latin American struggles, the 25-year-old Venezuelan, Simón Bolívar, agitated for independence in 1808 in Venezuela and then Columbia . Bolívar's crusade was initially repressed by Spanish loyalists, resulting in his exile in the West Indies. But he returned, indomitable, in 1817 and became the focal figure in mobilizing an alliance of rich landowners, urban interests, and the poor. Bolívar displayed the self-taught military skills worthy of a Hannibal in his epic campaigns to oust Spanish royalists, which carried him over the Andes deep into Peru and southern Chile. Sadly, his aspiration for a pan-Latin American republic broke down when local elites, who had been happy for him to expel the Spaniards, refused to give up local control. Suspicious of democracy in a largely illiterate continent, Bolívar saw himself as a natural leader, a dictator expressing the will of the people. Although sincere, his belief set a dangerous precedent for future generals to see themselves as national saviours. His hopes for Latin American unity were foiled by local elites he helped come to power against Spain and he bitterly remarked, "Those who made the revolution have ploughed the sea."

DESTABILIZED COLONIES

The Declaration of the Rights of Man in Paris in 1789 posed a dilemma for the French colonies, and particularly impacted the valuable West Indian islands, where a tiny white French-speaking elite ruled over black slaves and mixed race (mulatto) subordinates. Saint-Domingue, modern-day Haiti, produced almost half of France's hard currency earnings from its vast sugar plantations.

When news of the Revolution reached Haiti in 1790, a local mulatto was tortured to death for suggesting that the colony adopt the new rights established in France. The president of the local whites-only colonial assembly stated bluntly, "We have not brought half a million slaves from the coasts of Africa to make them into French citizens." On 22 August 1791 fighting erupted between white slave owners and French troops against slave rebels; many sugar plantations and factories were destroyed by bitter ex-slaves during the fighting, reverting the economy to a primitive state. After news of the king's execution in 1793 a republic was proclaimed. The French republic accepted the Haitian leader, Francois Dominique Toussaint, and until 1802 he was the effective ruler of Haiti, trying to establish an enlightened regime after such upheaval.

Napoleon's regime in France reversed the Republic's abolition of slavery. Toussaint was tricked into captivity and a war of national liberation broke out. Haitians appealed to the ideals of the French Revolution to demoralize the invaders, who were fighting under difficult and unhealthy conditions. Then in 1804 their new leader, Jean-Jacques Dessalines, parodied Napoleon by proclaiming himself emperor. Dessalines was a hero of the anti-colonial struggle but his harsh policies towards mixed race Haitians led to his assassination in 1806. Although independent Haiti provided a model of successful anti-colonial revolution, the destruction to sugar plantations and refineries reduced the once wealthy island to poverty. The unwillingness of the French to extend human rights to their black Haitian subjects sparked the savage Haitian revolt. Haiti's tragic post-colonial history shows how transferring the ideals of the French revolution proved easier said than done.

In Europe, Napoleon's success in overthrowing old monarchies and his attempt to impose puppet rulers like his brother Joseph on Spain in 1808 sparked mass resistance. In Spain, gentry and local clergy became the focal points of an emerging guerrilla movement against French occupation. An important element in the Spanish revolt was the self-proclaimed liberals who declared a constitution for Spain in 1812 and set the ideals of the French Revolution against the invaders. Guerrillas and liberals would prove to be the lasting legacy of Spanish resistance to Napoleon, outliving their Spanish context.

1790

October 1790
First slave revolt on Haiti against white elite

15 May 1791
France grants civil rights to free blacks

22 August 1791
Renewed rebellion on Haiti against slave owners

29 August 1793
Toussaint marks victory by abolishing slavery in Haiti

4 February 1794
France abolishes slavery – restored by Napoleon in May 1802

1800

7 April 1803
Toussaint dies in French prison

31 December 1803
Haiti declares independence from France

March 1808
Napoleon occupies Spain – Latin America set adrift from Spanish authority

1810

25 May 1810
Argentina sets up first independent government (junta)

5 July 1811
Bolívar inspires Venezuelan congress to declare independence

1811–19
Bolívar leads war of independence in Latin America.

1820

24 December 1824
Last Spanish loyalists accept Peru's independence

17 December 1830
Bolívar dies disappointed at failure to achieve Latin American unity

Russia 1917

The Russian Revolution in 1917, like the French Revolution, was closely observed as a model for the future with hope by some and fear by others around the world. The establishment of the world's first avowedly communist regime and its successful survival in the bitter civil war that followed Lenin's seizure of power in November 1917 made the Russian Revolution a landmark event.

Out of a spontaneous popular uprising against the discredited imperial regime, which broke out three years into World War I in February 1917, Russia saw an unprecedented radicalization of its situation as the previously marginal communists led by Vladimir Lenin moved to the centre of events because of their leader's intuitive understanding of the popular mood – and his rivals' failure to grasp public opinion or to organize themselves effectively to flout it.

Russia had been in flux for decades before 1917 as the imperial regime tried to reconcile modernization of the economy and armed forces to preserve Russia's status as a great power with the autocratic government which no Tsar wanted to renounce.

Dramatic social change in the decades before World War I destabilized Russian society. The mixture of Western technologies next door to antiquated agricultural techniques meant that Russia had the kind of uneven development that fuelled social and political protest in so many developing countries as the 20th century progressed. This was what made Lenin's revolution so influential from China to Latin America.

Ignoring the warnings of his advisers that another war would recreate the revolutionary conditions of 1905 (see p72), Tsar Nicholas II plunged Russia into World War I in 1914, confident that his forces would soon win and that long-term imperial goals, like seizing the Straits at Constantinople, would be achieved. To ordinary Russians, these ambitions were as irrelevant as the war over Manchuria a decade earlier, but Germany was an even more dangerous enemy than Japan had been in 1904–5.

AN UNTENABLE WAR

For three years the Russian army was forced back into the interior of the Russian empire by the Germans, suffering huge losses in men and weapons. Compounding such losses, the war effort was poorly organized. Even when enough munitions were produced, troops were ill-supplied because of unreliable

1 November 1894
Accession of Nicholas II

30 December 1916
Murder of Rasputin

26 March 1917 *Abolition of death penalty in new Russian Republic*

16 April 1917 *Lenin returns to Petrograd from Switzerland*

6–7 November 1917 *Red Guards storm Winter Palace – Soviet regime established*

16 June 1918 *Restoration of the death penalty in Soviet Russia*

1 August 1914
Outbreak of World War I – Petersburg renamed Petrograd

1915

15 March 1917 *Nicholas II abdicates – Republic proclaimed*
8 March 1917 *Women protesters on streets of Petrograd mark International Women's Day*
5 March 1917 *Protests begin in ration-queues in Petrograd*

3 March 1918 *Soviet Russia signs peace with Germany at Brest-Litovsk*

16 July 1918 *Murder of ex-tsar Nicholas II and family in Ekatarinburg*

The Tsarina's fostering of the disreputable holy man, Grigory Rasputin, was a key factor in undermining the imperial family's reputation.

transport. The railway was unable to supply both the war front and big cities. As a result, the capital, Petrograd (renamed from St Petersburg to make it sound less German), experienced acute food and fuel shortages by late 1916 and prices spiralled out of control.

Having taken over command of the army in 1915, Nicholas II bore the blame for defeats while his German-born wife, Alexandra, was left in charge of the capital. Both Tsar and Tsarina were dangerously isolated from public opinion and oblivious to the growing internal crisis. In particular, they trusted the bogus holyman, Rasputin, who seemed to exert a strange influence over their ailing son's haemophilia. False rumours about the Tsarina's relationship with Rasputin and truthful stories about his corruption compounded bad news from the front and hardships at home to discredit the imperial family. In December 1916 disaffected aristocrats murdered Rasputin, triggering the country's slide into revolution.

In early March 1917 workers in Petrograd protested against the imperial regime. Overwhelmed by the crowds, the police called out troops. However the soldiers joined the protesters on 8 March. Officers trying to stop the mutiny were shot by their men and Petrograd was controlled by revolutionaries.

The Tsar tried to return to Petrograd to suppress the disorder but was prevented from doing so by striking railway workers. Faced by mutinies and strikes, and abandoned by his own generals, Nicholas II abdicated. His son and brother also renounced the throne and overnight Russia became a republic.

Moderate liberal and socialist members of the Duma, the Russian parliament, were catapulted into ministerial posts as members

---

May 1920
Civil War ends with fall of
Crimea – Whites flee abroad

January 1924
Death of Lenin

December 1928
First Five-Year Plan
proclaimed – forced
collectivization

1929
Exile of Trotsky

March 1921 Kronstadt rebellion suppressed. Communist
Party proclaims New Economic Policy (NEP)

20 December 1929
Stalin's 50th birthday
celebrated – start of cult
of personality

1930

of the provisional government. Bewildered by the scale of the problems facing Russia, they misread the popular mood. As educated men, ministers like Alexander Kerensky looked to history for models of what to do. Only the French Revolution seemed to provide an obvious precedent for what was happening in Russia as the old order fell away. Hadn't the French Republic rallied support in a war of defence against the very Germans and Austrians now invading Russia?

Unfortunately for the provisional government, the mood of Russia in 1917 was very different from France in 1792. War-weariness gripped the country. One Russian politician to sense the popular mood was Vladimir Lenin, who was exiled in Switzerland when the revolution broke out.

Stalin, Lenin and Kalinin (l–r). Lenin relied on shrewd tactics to gain control over the soviets, recognizing their potential to challenge the provisional government.

The Germans saw troublemaking potential in his tiny radical party, so they returned Lenin to Russia in a sealed train (like a "plague bacillus" according to Winston Churchill). When he arrived in Petrograd in April 1917, Lenin attempted to undermine the provisional government and war effort.

Lenin used slogans such as "Peace, land, and bread" and "All power to the soviets" to appeal to the hungry and disillusioned masses. He also recognized the importance of the soldiers' and workers' councils, or soviets, which had sprung up everywhere since February and their potential in challenging the provisional government. By emphasizing that the soviets were more representative of the Russian people than the provisional government, Lenin aimed to establish a parallel power structure.

To gain control of the soviets, bodies which often had no formal rules or membership,

Lenin used shrewd tactics. He held an iron grip over his own majority or Bolshevik wing of the revolutionary Marxist Russian Social Democrats. Now he used his supporters to infiltrate the soviets. Lenin's hostility to the war attracted many recruits to his cause. In fact, before Lenin returned to Russia, the Petrograd soviet had already challenged the new provisional government by passing its first resolution, stating that troops in the capital's garrison could only be sent to the front with the soviet's permission.

Throughout 1917 the war continued and inflation, food shortages, and casualties alienated people from the provisional government. By the end of October, Lenin's party had increased to 225,000 activists. Its militia, the Red Guards, was ready to seize Petrograd. Meanwhile the provisional government's support had dwindled. Although Lenin had the best organized party, popular support for his communist aims paled next to the Russian people's disillusionment with the provisional government. In fact, in the elections to the Constituent Assembly that was called to draw up the constitution of a new Russia, Lenin's party received only about 25 per cent of the vote, while the rest of Russia was divided and passive. Even so, Lenin recognized that most people would not oppose him, so on 6 November 1917 Lenin's Red Guards stormed the provisional government's headquarters at the Winter Palace in Petrograd. Only a handful of officer cadets and women soldiers put up a half-hearted defence.

A NEW SOVIET STATE

Although Lenin's published pamphlet, *State and Revolution*, argued that after a proletarian revolution the state's police and bureaucrats would disappear, soon after his coup Lenin set up a new secret police, the Cheka, to combat any counter-revolutionary opposition. Also, Lenin's government did not allow workers' self-management in industry and was so anxious to get production back under way that former capitalist managers were allowed to run factories as "bourgeois experts".

To keep the population calm while the new Soviet government established itself, Lenin and his chief aide, Trotsky, issued two important decrees calling on the warring states to make peace and telling the Russian peasants to divide the land among themselves.

The Decree on Land was a shrewd means of scattering the only force capable of challenging Russia's new self-proclaimed rulers. As Lenin had expected, the army fell apart when its peasant soldiers ran home to take part in the division of land. Lenin made peace with Germany.

In March 1918, Lenin agreed to the harsh terms of the Treaty of Brest-Litovsk, conceding vast areas of western Russia to Germany and her allies. Although it was a bitter pill to swallow, Lenin was convinced that he had saved the revolution. In fact, he was hopeful that countries like Germany would soon follow the Soviet model. As a Marxist, Lenin believed that communist revolutions would occur naturally in the most industrialized and urban societies in the world, where more than half the population consisted of the industrial working class. The Russian revolution was an anomaly for Lenin because it occurred in a largely rural society, but he felt that would soon be rectified by the westward spread of revolution to more advanced states like Germany, who would then help to modernize Russia.

Whatever Lenin expected, in the spring of 1918 anti-communist White forces, largely composed of former imperial army officers who viewed Lenin's peace with Germany as treason but who were also deeply hostile to communism, rallied on the fringes of Russia. They received support from Britain, France, and America, who viewed Lenin's government as a German puppet due to its withdrawal from the war.

But the Whites were disadvantaged in the civil war that ensued. Lenin's supporters controlled the core of European Russia, based in Moscow, which now became the capital of the Soviet state. Using the resources of cities like Moscow and Petrograd, Trotsky built up the Red Army to a three-million-strong force. The White armies scattered around Russia could never deploy such numbers and had difficulty coordinating their operations across vast distances.

WHITES CRUSHED

The White generals controlled the politics of their areas but were poor propagandists. Even though they had no intention of restoring the unpopular Tsar

Nicholas II or serfdom, which most peasants feared, the generals made no serious effort to counter communist claims to the contrary. By contrast, Lenin and Trotsky offered populist slogans playing on the fears of the masses.

Nonetheless the civil war was bitter. Both sides committed atrocities to terrorize opponents into submission, and the ex-Imperial family was murdered in July 1918 to show the Red Army there could be no turning back: defeat would mean suffering terrible revenge. The civil war wrecked the economy further and famine spread through much of central Russia as troops robbed the peasants, taking the food they needed and destroying the rest of the crops to keep them from the enemy.

By mid-1920, the Red Army had crushed the Whites, capturing their last stronghold, the Crimea. But the revolution was not yet over. In fact, in Lenin's eyes it had hardly begun. He hoped to abolish private property and capitalism completely, and replace them with a socialist economy, while envisioning a modern industrialized Russia. His slogan was "Communism = soviet power plus electrification of the whole country." However, the defeat of the Whites brought discontent from unexpected quarters.

As a step to communism, Lenin had tried to abolish money while still giving preferential treatment to key members of the new communist regime. This did not stop with the end of the civil war and many ordinary Soviet supporters felt betrayed by this privileged group, the so-called nomenklatura.

Peasants across Russia had also come to hate the abuses of the Red Army. They had not supported the Whites, their former landlords, but they now formed peasant "Green" forces to fight the Reds. Trotsky was ruthless in smashing rural opposition. Meanwhile in March 1921 sailors and dockyard workers in Kronstadt near Petrograd, who had been the spearhead of the November 1917 revolution, "the reddest of the red" Lenin had once called them, now rose up against what they decried as the dictatorship of Lenin's "red bourgeoisie." But the Red Army's officers sided with Lenin and smashed the Kronstadt Rising.

"Long live the fifth anniversary of the Great Proletarian Revolution!" (1922). Repression and regimentation from 1918–21 helped fuel the rise of Stalin after Lenin's death.

Marxists had called for the proletariat to replace the tsarist autocracy, but now a dictatorship by the Communist Party over the proletariat was established. The Soviet state took shape amidst civil war and international isolation, but its methods and attitudes lasted for decades. Suspicion of outsiders, internal repression, and regimentation of everyday life ingrained in the 1918–21 period aided the rise of Stalin after Lenin's death in 1924.

Failed Revolutions 1918

Defeat in World War I spelled revolution not only for Russia but also for the Central European monarchies. Only three republics existed in Europe before the war; afterwards there were 13. But in post-war defeat and economic chaos the new states proved highly unstable while establishing themselves.

War-weary and mutinous servicemen played a key role in toppling the German emperor and Austro-Hungarian empire in November 1918, bringing the Marxist Lenin to leadership. But opponents of radical political and social transformation swiftly moved to suppress the radical left in Central Europe.

The new Soviet regime hoped to turn the Russian revolution into a global one and set up the Communist International (Comintern) in Moscow in March 1919 to coordinate the activity of Communist Parties around the world. Technically, all the Communist Parties constituted one global party with national "sections" and, despite inadequate communication, the Kremlin directed their activities. Kremlin control proved counter-productive in two ways: Moscow's instructions often conflicted with practical regional realities and such Russian control inflamed anti-communist propaganda.

Due to its size, Germany was the linchpin in any Soviet expansion in Central Europe. With a collapsed monarchy and a republic proclaimed on 9 November 1918, Germany seemed to be moving in the Russian direction. But Germany's workers' councils, or soviets, were not organized like Lenin's communists for a para-military revolutionary struggle. In fact, the radical German Marxist, Rosa Luxemburg, actually criticized the new Soviet state's intolerance of dissent. Even so, the German right viewed her as a Marxist and thus Lenin-sympathizer. In 1919 an ex-officer death squad murdered Luxemburg and Karl Liebknecht, a close comrade.

Right-wing reactionaries studied the Russian revolution, spurring on the rapid emergence of right-wing paramilitary groups like the one that killed Luxemburg. Lenin succeeded as a Marxist leader partly because, as the first, his rivals did not understand his way of politics. A year later in Germany reactionary army officers and moderate Social Democrat leaders cooperated to battle the radical left, which tried to stage a Bolshevik-style seizure of power at the end of 1918. To German communists, the social democrats were class traitors and a bitter internal left-wing feud began, which played a part in Hitler's rise to power 14 years later.

The country that came closest to a successful communist revolution was Hungary. In the instability following Hungary's break with Austria in early 1919, Bela Kun, who had learned about communism while an ex-prisoner of war in Russia, succeeded in mobilizing workers in big industrial centres, especially the capital, Budapest, to support local communists. A Soviet republic was proclaimed and briefly it appeared that the leadership of the old social order, made up of both the urban elite and rural landowners, would collapse. While the economy worsened under Bela Kun, the Hungarian right rallied military veterans and reactionary volunteers to combat the communist regime. The Allies' sent troops to aid the right and by August 1919, the Hungarian Soviet experiment collapsed in a welter of violence.

The fact that several leading communist revolutionaries, like Rosa Luxemburg in Germany or Bela Kun in Hungary, were of Jewish descent fanned the flames of anti-Semitism. Radical counter-revolutionaries alleged that communism was part of a Jewish plot. Racism and reaction marched hand in hand, finding a voice in the post-World War generation that supported the 30-year-old Adolf Hitler, who made his first unsuccessful attempt to seize power on the anniversary of the revolution in 1923 in the Beer Hall Putsch.

Association with the Soviet model did not help Central European Marxists. More than two million refugees fled the Russian revolution to the West and their stories of communist atrocities helped to stimulate counter-revolutionary groups determined to avoid the same fate. Also, for many the Soviet regime was just another form of Russian domination. When Russia's Red Army advanced into Poland in 1920, instead of being greeted as liberators by workers and peasants, the invasion was bitterly resisted and defeated in August 1920 – an omen of the failure of communism to establish a loyal constituency in Eastern Europe after 1945.

1915

1920

1925

- **4 November 1918** German Navy mutiny
- **9 November 1918** Kaiser Wilhelm flees – republic proclaimed
- **19 December 1918** Germans vote for parliament rather than Soviet-style republic
- **23 December 1918** Berlin uprising begins
- **15 January 1919** Marxist revolutionary, Rosa Luxemburg, murdered
- **19 January 1919** German parliamentary elections
- **21 March 1919** Bela Kun proclaims Soviet republic in Hungary
- **6 April 1919** Short-lived Soviet republic in Bavaria
- **1 August 1919** Bela Kun flees collapse of Hungarian Soviet republic
- **11 August 1923** Right-wing Gustav Stresemann appointed German Chancellor – followed by widespread Marxist demonstrations
- **2 November 1923** German Army acts against communists in Thuringia
- **9 November 1923** Hitler's Beer Hall Putsch fails in Munich

Germany 1933

On 30 January 1933 Adolf Hitler was appointed to the office of German Chancellor. Although completely legal, the event represented the culmination of a gathering tide of counter-revolution. Hitler and his National Socialist German Workers Party were not only violently anti-communist, they openly rejected the heritage of the French Revolution with its Declaration of the Rights of Man. After the Nazis took office, their propaganda chief, Dr Josef Goebbels, announced, "The year 1789 is hereby eradicated from history", implying that the French Revolution's universalist ideals of human rights and equality had been replaced by the Nazis' racist and elitist vision.

A RACIST COUNTER-REVOLUTION

The coming to power of the Nazis was the prelude to a 12-year attempt at a racist counter-revolution that plunged Europe and then the world into the most destructive and horrific war in history. Adolf Hitler's radical ideological goals were little understood before 1933, and even the parallels between his rise to power and Mussolini's in Italy were generally discounted. Hitler was underestimated by both his domestic rivals

and right-wing groups who hoped to use the Nazi movement to serve their own ends.

Looking back before the so-called Third Reich (empire) was established helps to explain how key groups in German society before 1933 cooperated with or ignored the dangers posed by Hitler's Nazis. Like other fascistic movements, the paramilitary, radically right-wing Nazi Party had emerged in the post-war conditions of 1919 when defeat meant territorial loss, economic dislocation, and bitter resentment for millions of Germans. As an ex-frontline soldier himself, Adolf Hitler, like many, felt that Germany's post-war difficulties after 1919 had been caused by the injustices of the Treaty of Versailles and the betrayal of Germany's national interests by the democratic and left-wing politicians who had accepted it. But Hitler also knew how to manipulate the confusion and resentment of his contemporaries, persuading them to accept extreme racist and aggressive ideas.

Having failed to seize power in the Beer Hall Putsch in 1923, Hitler adopted the path of legality and his Nazi Party took part in elections. Few understood how cynically the Nazis intended to exploit what Goebbels called the "arsenal of democracy" to destroy

20 April 1889
Birth of Adolf Hitler

I August 1914 Outbreak of World War I

II November 1918 Germany accepts armistice to end World War I

1900

1909 Adolf Hitler moves to Germany from Austria to avoid military service

1915

9 November 1918 Collapse of German Empire – Kaiser Wilhelm flees

German Olympic athletes salute the Führer at the XI Olympic Games in Berlin, 1936. Gold-medal winner Jesse Owens, an African American, was not congratulated by Hitler on his win.

it. If membership of parliament gave them immunity from arrest and free rail travel, then Hitler and his comrades would use it to promote their own radical agenda, which involved the abolition of democracy and the rule of law.

Until the Great Depression in 1929, Hitler, a militaristic clown figure, and his dictatorial ambitions seemed laughable to rivals. But within a year of the economic downturn, the nearly seven million unemployed were giving Hitler's message a hearing. In 1930, the Nazis became the second largest party with 18 per cent of the votes; by mid-1932 they were the biggest with 37 per cent.

Driven to despair by the ever-deepening economic crisis, others turned to the Communist Party. In 1932, more than half the German electorate voted for the two anti-democratic parties, which gave them a paralyzing majority in the Reichstag (German parliament). No laws could be passed without their agreement, and they agreed to very little. Both Nazis and communists hoped to benefit from the growing tension and despair. The electoral annihilation of moderate parties and the shrinkage of the

9 November 1923
Hitler's failed Beer Hall Putsch in Munich

27 February 1933
Reichstag Fire – Hitler's excuse to ban Communists

30 June 1934 Night of the Long Knives – Hitler eliminates Nazi rivals
2 August 1934 President von Hindenburg dies – Hitler assumes power

9 November 1939
"Kristallnacht" – pogrom against Germany's Jews

28 June 1919 Germany signs Treaty of Versailles admitting war guilt"

1930

2 May 1933 Trades unions banned – only Nazi Labour Front allowed
30 January 1933 Adolf Hitler appointed Chancellor of Germany

23 August 1939 Nazi-Soviet Pact signed in Moscow – green light for war

1945

Social Democrats, formerly the bastion of the democratic Weimar Republic, paved the way to the collapse of democracy.

The Nazis garnered more support because of their combination of promises to put people back to work and their cunning ability to play on the German people's resentment of the Versailles Treaty, while the communists were too pro-Russian and unpatriotic for many. Hitler turned out to be a charismatic public speaker who could elicit an extraordinary emotional and aggressive response from his audience. The radio, then cinema newsreels, gave Hitler media he could exploit to carry his message. The democratic politicians seemed out of their depth in dealing with the Depression and were unable to control the atmosphere of near civil war generated by uniformed Nazi storm troopers fighting to control the streets of Germany against communist paramilitaries.

With ranks of storm troopers and millions of voters, Hitler came close to achieving high office, but since his support fell short of a parliamentary majority, he needed help outside the Nazi Party to cross the threshold of the Reich Chancellery. A small group of aristocratic string-pullers around the aged President von Hindenburg played a vital role in arranging Hitler's legal appointment as chancellor at the end of January 1933. Also businessmen were reassured that the word "socialist" in the Nazi Party's title would not mean expropriation of private property.

A photomontage by John Heartfield, 14 April 1937, entitled Die Saat des Todes (The Seeds of Death), *depicting the ruinous impact of the Nazis.*

HITLER APPOINTED CHANCELLOR

Like many of the conventional German right-wing politicians, Franz von Papen and his friend, President von Hindenburg's son, Oskar, underrated the former corporal, Hitler. Preoccupied with countering the communist threat and forgetting what had happened in Italy a decade earlier, Papen and his friends thought they could use Hitler and his followers as a weapon to destroy the radical left and then drop them.

Die Saat des Todes

Within days of persuading Hindenburg to appoint a Hitler-led government on 30 January, Papen was out-manoeuvred by Hitler. Although Nazis only held four ministerial posts, they were the key ones, with Hitler as chancellor and the others in charge of the police and interior, plus Goebbels at the newly created Ministry of Propaganda and Public Enlightenment. Using the police and storm troopers, the new regime prepared for fresh elections on 6 March 1933 by a wholesale assault on both communists and Social Democrats.

COMMUNISTS ELIMINATED

Despite using the legal electoral process, it was not clear that the German voters would return a clear Nazi majority. Whether by chance or by design, on 28 February Hitler received a godsend, the German Parliament went up in flames and the man captured on the spot – a Dutchman, Marinus van der Lubbe, who had communist connections – was accused of starting the fire. Hindenburg decreed a state of emergency, allowing the police to arrest communist candidates and activists. Sinister concentration camps were established to hold these political prisoners at places like Dachau outside Munich.

Even under an unprecedented propaganda barrage that was backed by widespread intimidation the Nazis polled only 43 per cent of the vote. With the eight per cent support for their right-wing allies, Hitler had a working majority, but he wanted total power. Keeping the communist deputies

under arrest, Hitler bullied and bribed members of the Reichstag to pass an enabling act that gave him, as chancellor, dictatorial powers for four years.

Within weeks left-wing parties and trade unions had been banned and the more conservative ones dissolved out of fear of reprisals. From mid-summer 1933, all organizations, from the labour force to sports clubs, could only exist if affiliated with the Nazi Party. Jews, the objects of Hitler's venom, faced discrimination, boycotts, and violence from the storm troopers, egged on by Goebbels' anti-Semitic propaganda.

Having silenced all opposition, Hitler now faced a challenge from within the Party. Many of the storm-trooper Brownshirts took the socialist rhetoric of the Nazis just as seriously as the nationalist demands. Led by the storm-trooper leader, Ernst Roehm, they demanded a merging of the aristocrat-run army with storm troopers and other measures, which threatened to destabilize Hitler's smooth working relationship with the conservative German establishment.

On 30 June 1934, Hitler lashed out at Roehm and his allies. Accusing them of plotting a coup d'état, and blackening their reputations with allegations of homosexuality and corruption, Hitler had Roehm and about 60 others shot without trial. In addition to the dissident Nazis, former Chancellor von Schleicher and even the proofreader of *Mein Kampf*, Hitler's programmatic book, were shot. It was a clear sign that anyone who challenged Hitler would face death.

Within weeks, President von Hindenburg died and Hitler assumed office and the rank of commander-in-chief of the armed forces, whose soldiers now swore a personal oath of loyalty to Adolf Hitler as "Führer" or Leader of Germany. Power was concentrated in Hitler's hands in a way Mussolini never achieved in Italy.

AN EXPANSIONIST PLAN

Ordinary Germans remained quiet through these bloody and illegal events, partly out of fear, and partly because Hitler had instinctively grasped a way out of the Depression. While democratic governments had tried to balance their budgets with spending cuts that made economic conditions worse, Hitler embarked on huge expansionist road-building schemes and the building up of the armed forces. Spending on weapons and conscription after 1935 helped reduce unemployment dramatically. For millions of ex-unemployed, turning a blind eye to the Nazis' growing persecution of Jews and other minorities was made easier by renewed economic well-being.

Still in the Depression, and with their public opinion hostile to any new war which might revive the horrors of the trenches, Britain and France let Hitler flout the Treaty of Versailles and take over Austria and then German-speaking Sudetenland from Czechoslovakia without opposition by September 1938.

Domestic and foreign success did not moderate Hitler. The most brutal pogrom yet of the Nazi period erupted on 9 November 1938. The so-called Kristallnacht ("Night of Broken Glass") saw synagogues and other Jewish property ransacked by storm troopers and thousands of German Jews imprisoned in concentration camps. To add insult to injury the Nazis accused them of causing the damage and fined the Jewish community a billion marks. It was a sign that Hitler's anti-Semitism would not be toned down by success.

By mid-March 1939, it was clear that Hitler would not abide by his promise only to seek unification with Germans since he occupied the remaining Czech territory left independent. Then he demanded concessions from Poland. Finally, Britain and France stood up to Hitler, only to find that Stalin's Soviet Union had made a secret deal to avoid war in August 1939. Hitler invaded Poland at the start of September, but this time the Western democracies declared war.

Although the Nazi armies quickly overran Poland and Western Europe by mid-summer 1940, Britain held out. Deluded by his triumphs, Hitler ignored the risk of a two-front war like World War I, and decided to fulfil his life-long ambition to destroy communism in the land of its birth. On 22 June 1941, the German army invaded the Soviet Union. In spite of early victories and huge Soviet casualties, a prolonged war of attrition in terrible winter conditions began to wear the German army down.

Thousands of Jews and others persecuted by the Nazis were herded through the gates of Auschwitz, one of the infamous concentration camps in Poland.

THE ALLIES FIGHT BACK

As Hitler recognized that victory in war would not be easily achieved, if at all, his vengefulness turned against powerless civilian victims. The so-called "Final Solution of the Jewish Question" through mass murder grew in terrifying scale as the tide of the war turned against Nazi Germany. Unable to resist the Allies' strength, the Nazi regime herded more and more defenceless Jews from occupied Europe into death camps, especially in occupied Poland, where up to six million people were worked to death, gassed, or shot.

Aggression and racial purity were key themes of Hitler's ideology. He pursued them regardless of the consequences. Hitler's obsessive anti-Semitism remained with him to the end. Even as he was besieged in his bunker in Berlin by the Soviet Army in late April 1945, only hours before his suicide he was urging imaginary successors to continue his anti-Jewish crusade.

The complete defeat of Nazi Germany in 1945 led to an implosion of the Nazi Party and ideology. Unlike countries occupied by Germany between 1938 and 1945, Germany itself produced no resistance movement to Allied occupation. Hitler's death and the destruction he had brought down on Germany itself as well as the rest of Europe had exorcized his influence.

China 1911–49

The Chinese communist leader, Mao Zedong, proclaimed the People's Republic of China on 1 October 1949, marking the climax of an extraordinary set of changes which shattered the age-old imperial system that had ruled China. The deposition of the last emperor in February 1912 marked the end of one revolution and the beginning of a series of frequently violent events that shook the world's most populous society for the next six decades.

Since China opened its doors to the West at the end of the 18th century, foreign contact crucially impacted the country and influenced the republican revolution of 1911. Foreign predators and their superior military technology revealed the profound internal weaknesses of the time-honoured and no longer infallible imperial system.

DYNASTY LOSES ITS GRIP

Torn between trying to learn from the Western powers and anxiety to preserve their own ancient ways, by the end of the

Created by a teachers' collective at the Central Institute for Fine Arts, this painting depicts China's Heroes of our Time.

19th century, the ruling Manchu dynasty's hold on power was weakening constantly. It seemed the "mandate of heaven" no longer protected its succession of juvenile-rulers, none of whom was a suitable imperial strongman capable of effective government. The fact that key decisions were made by advisers under the shadowy influence of the Dowager Empress until her death in 1908 simply added to the sense that the traditional order was hopelessly out of kilter. Efforts by the traditionally minded secret

1839–42 British victory in Opium wars humiliates imperial China	**1895** Japan humiliates China in short war over Korea and Taiwan	**12 February 1912** Abdication of the last emperor, Pu-Yi	**1913** Sun Yatsen elected first President of China	**July 1921** Chinese Communist Party established in Shanghai

1850–64 The Taiping revolution convulses much of central China   **1910**   **10 October 1911** Soldiers mutiny in Wuhan – start of revolution   **4 May 1919** Students demonstrate in Beijing against Japanese imperialism   **1925**

12 March 1925 Death of Sun Yatsen

societies to destroy foreign influence by attacking Westerners in 1900, had backfired when foreign troops squashed the rebellion and made clear the impotence of the imperial government. Command by Beijing over the provinces began to break down as local military leaders took control for themselves. At the same time, Chinese intellectuals who had been influenced by Western ideas began to press for constitutional reform and socio-economic changes to the traditional order.

The most prominent intellectual reformer was the American-educated Dr Sun Yatsen, who had become a Christian. His political ideology was "Nationalism, Democracy, Socialism". He established what became the Chinese Nationalist Party, the Kuomintang (KMT), as far back as 1891.

MUTINY MAKES WAY FOR CHANGE

If imperial China was to survive foreign pressures it was clear that a modern army would be central to any reform effort in China. By 1911, key groups of officers in the new Western-style army had decided that the Manchu dynasty was incapable of saving the country. In October 1911, a group of nationalist officers in Wuhan openly rebelled by cutting off their pigtails, which were signs of subservience to the Manchu, in protest

when the regime granted Western interests control of the new railways as surety for loans – an act that symbolized the country had sold out the national interest to foreigners. Nationalism was a key ingredient in Chinese discontent as it had been since the great peasant Taiping rebellion in the 1850s.

Within months of the Wuhan mutiny, the last emperor, the five-year-old Pu-Yi, abdicated in February 1912, which was an after-thought since political power had already passed from him. Sun Yatsen was elected first president of China in 1913, but army commanders who fancied themselves as new emperors challenged his powers.

NEW REGIME THREATENED

Already in 1913, the Five Powers – Britain, France, Germany, Japan and Russia – loaned money to a rebellious general, Yuan Shi-kai, and backed his claim to re-establish an imperial system. Foreigners had no interest in a reformed, modernized China, even one that wanted to follow Western models. They saw it as a potential rival.

Japan was as ruthless towards China as any of the European imperial powers or the United States. In 1915, while the Europeans were fighting World War I, Japan issued her notorious 21 Demands to the fledgling Chinese Republic, which would have subordinated China's foreign and economic policies to Japan. It became clear the West would do little to protect China from its ally, Japan, and on 4 May 1919, Beijing students held a pro-democracy and national independence rally. Only about 3,000 people participated but it became a symbolic moment of resistance to national humiliation. It has continued to resonate throughout Chinese history and was celebrated by huge crowds in 1989, then demonstrating against the communist regime in power.

FIRST CONGRESS OF COMMUNIST PARTY

The Fourth of May Movement also helped spawn the Chinese Communist Party. If the West had abandoned China, it had also isolated Soviet Russia. Lenin's increasingly successful attempt to set up a new type of society, which defied not only Russian traditions but also the powerful Western Allies, was attractive to many Chinese, including those who did not advocate the abandonment of private property but wanted to modernize China and defend their society against alien encroachments.

In July 1921, a few Chinese Marxists met, ironically, at a private girls' school in the French-ruled concession in Shanghai. Their meeting – in retrospect – became the first congress of the Chinese Communist Party. At first the new Communist Party was part of the Kuomintang, and Sun Yatsen saw no contradiction in that since he wanted Soviet help for the Chinese Republic.

The Soviet Union saw both the fledgling Chinese Communist Party and the Kuomintang movement as allies against the West and Japan. The Kremlin gave both groups aid, though for the next 15 years most of its aid when to the larger

Kuomintang with its formal control of the armed forces. Soviet military advisers taught the young General Chiang Kaishek's men the principles of modern mechanized warfare alongside German experts who also wanted to back an anti-Western China after 1918.

The Soviet revolutionary coordination centre, the Comintern, advised Chinese communists to enter the Kuomintang and to influence politics through it. The First KMT was held at the end of January 1924, and news of Lenin's death arrived during the sessions, so that Sun Yatsen could use the news to emphasize his organization's sympathy for the Soviet Union because of the KMT's "anti-imperialism". Sun Yatsen himself died in March 1925, and his death removed the one politician respected by the KMT mainstream and communists alike. Sun's successor was the army commander, Chiang Kaishek, a bad sign for China's chances of developing democratically.

At the end of April 1927, the orthodox Marxist leader, Chen Tu-hsiu, who believed that the Communist Party should focus its recruitment in the coastal cities where something like a working class existed, was murdered along with thousands of urban communists in a sudden purge by Chiang's secret police and allied Triad gangs. Chen's death left the way open to the young ex-librarian, Mao Zedong, to come to the fore. Mao, who came from a peasant family, saw the vast mass of Chinese peasants as a potential well of support for a revolutionary party that advocated the end of landlordism.

By the beginning of 1929, Chiang Kaishek seemed to have subdued the whole of China and made it recognize a single government for the first time since 1911, but in fact his rule was shallow. Many warlords had formally accepted his government in Nanking, but in practice controlled much of the country, and in south-east China rural communists made headway, setting up large "liberated zones".

THE LONG MARCH

In the early 1930s, Chiang used the Soviet training against the Chinese communists. His forces surrounded the communist-controlled region of Kiangsi in the south. Eventually in the autumn of 1934, the besieged communists made a bold break out of the encirclement and embarked on what became the legendary Long March.

The hardships and dangers of the Long March whittled the original 100,000 communists and families to barely 8,000 people by the time they reached sanctuary in Yunan. They had overcome not only the KMT and warlord forces but crossed fast-flowing rivers, climbed mountains, and marched through unmapped swamps, more than 6,000 miles in total. A tight bond was created among the survivors. Even child participants – like the future premier in 1989, Li Peng, whose parents died on the march and who was adopted by Mao's future premier, Chou En-lai – were treated with special respect afterwards.

A NEW GUERRILLA ARMY

Secure in their new base, the communists led by Mao built up the infrastructure of their revolutionary regime, imposing land reform and training a new guerrilla army. With their radical doctrine of rural warfare, the People's Liberation Army aimed to isolate the KMT-held towns in a sea of revolutionary peasants. This model of a peasant-led/nationalist revolution would be imitated later in Vietnam.

The Japanese invasion of China in 1937 destabilized the KMT's position. Steadily, at huge cost to the Chinese people, the Japanese forces drove Chiang's troops out of the big coastal cities and further back into the remote south-western region centred on Chunking by 1944. Many of Chiang's supporters – local officials, landowners, or businessmen especially – fled with the KMT

troops. Those who remained tended to collaborate with the Japanese and to leave the only guerrilla resistance force in the hands of Mao's communists. Because the Japanese advance continued almost to the end of the war in August 1945, despite America's victories in the Pacific theatre and the devastating bombing of Japan, almost all the most populous and economically valuable parts of China were occupied by Japan when the atomic bomb suddenly and inevitably produced her surrender.

With the aid of US airplanes, Chiang raced to deploy troops into Japanese-controlled areas where the occupying Japanese troops were told to remain on guard and await their arrival. This contributed to the portrayal of the KMT by the communists as Japanese

A member of the Mao Zedong Thought Propaganda Team promotes the leader at the No. 31 Middle School in Beijing , 1971.

collaborators, and foreigners as enemies of Chinese interests.

Although the Kuomintang was officially a revolutionary force in its own right, by the late 1940s it had become hopelessly corrupt. Its corruption undermined its power base even in natural centres of support like the big commercial cities on the coast. Another problem was wartime hyperinflation, which actually worsened after 1945. As the value of money crashed, so did support for the KMT among business circles.

The People's Liberation Army recovered from Chiang's early attacks and began to exploit the KMT's unpopularity and military incompetence. KMT troops showed little will to fight and in 1948 the PLA made staggering advances, capturing Beijing in January 1949.

In January 1949, Chiang resigned as president, but stayed on as leader of the KMT and supervised the withdrawal of hundreds of thousands of his loyalists to Taiwan, where they could be protected from the PLA by the US Navy's seventh fleet.

A PEOPLE'S REPUBLIC OF CHINA

The rapid collapse of KMT forces on the mainland meant that by the end of September 1949, for the first time in many decades, the whole of China was controlled by one government. The PLA's victory fulfilled the nationalist part of the communists' agenda. The importance of Mao's anti-imperialist Chinese nationalism was emphasized in his speech proclaiming the establishment of the People's Republic of China in Beijing on 1 October 1949. Having announced the communist victory, Mao declared, "Today, China has stood up."

What kind of China Mao and his comrades intended to create only became evident in the coming three decades. At first it was the landlords who suffered as about one million were killed in the post-revolutionary period. However within a decade, hundreds of millions of Chinese peasants, who had received land at the end of the 1940s, were dispossessed to make way for Mao's over-ambitious development scheme, the ill thought out Great Leap Forward (1958–61), which disrupted food production in the quest to make China industrialized overnight and caused tens of millions to starve to death. As he grew older and more dogmatic, Mao fell out with the Soviet Union, and then with former comrades-in-arms. In 1966 he launched the Cultural Revolution to purify the Communist Party of alleged backsliders from his pure doctrines. This lasted until his death in 1976. China's history since then has been marked by the ruling Communist Party's attempts to undo the effects of Mao's radical last years without losing power itself.

The greatest challenge to the Chinese Communist regime came in the spring of 1989 when hundreds of thousands of students and then workers filled Beijing's central Tiananmen Square to denounce corruption and demand democracy. The regime responded with force and quelled the protests, but it could not take its own stability for granted again.

Iran 1978-9

The Iranian Revolution that established the Islamic Republic in 1979 was one of the most remarkable modern revolutions because it seemed to overturn the trend towards secularization in the 20th century. Until the fall of the Shah of Iran, revolutions had been associated with a commitment to the ideals of progress and breaking with the past. Suddenly, in 1979, a revolution motivated by religious faith and led by an aged cleric who denounced the key tenets of the modern world swept all before it.

A VALUABLE ALLY

Oil-rich Iran was situated in one of the world's most strategically sensitive zones. To its north lay the Soviet Union. To the south was the Persian Gulf, the seaway for the export of the vast petroleum resources of Iraq and the Arab states along its shore to North America, Europe, and Japan. Westwards beyond Iraq and Jordan was Israel, the focus of so much tension in the Middle East. As the Cold War developed after 1945, Iran's resources and location made her extremely valuable to the US, which was determined to keep a pro-Western government in power

there as a vital requirement of its foreign policy. Unfortunately, although the country proved to be an invaluable ally to the West, it also maintained a regime that oppressed most Iranians.

THE SHAH IS EXILED

Iran had been convulsed by political crises since the early 20th century when the ancient imperial regime collapsed, but the establishment of a military dictatorship under the self-proclaimed Shah Reza Pahlavi in 1928 brought stability. His harsh regime then began to exploit the country's oil resources. When the British government and British oil companies operating there suspected Shah Reza of plotting to join the Germans in World War II, they engineered his forced retirement into exile, putting his young son, Reza II on the throne.

A PUPPET OF FOREIGN POWERS

When American influence replaced British power after the war, the infant CIA, (Central Intelligence Agency), played a key role in keeping the shah in power in 1953 when the popular nationalist premier Mossadeq

16 September 1941 Shah's father deposed by British and the young Mohammed Reza Pahlavi installed as ruler of Iran

16–19 August 1953 CIA-organized coup brings the shah back to Iran after a brief exile

1940

May 1951–August 1953 Power struggle between shah and nationalist premier, Mossadeq

1955

November 1964 Ayatollah Khomeini exiled to Iraq

This anti-shah demonstration in front of the Iranian embassy in Paris was called by the French Communist Party in 1979.

seemed about to topple him and nationalize the oil fields. The CIA waged a covert war against the Soviet Union and its allies in Iran, regarding anyone who opposed the shah and Western domination in the Gulf as a Soviet stooge. By the early 1950s, the West was increasingly dependent on imported oil from the Middle East, and feared that a radical leader like Mossadeq would cut supplies or massively increase prices. The sinister and self-interested role of America in keeping the unpopular shah in power confirmed his reputation as a puppet of foreign and non-Muslim powers. Although the CIA thought it was saving Iran from Soviet-style communism, in fact a powerful traditional Muslim hostility towards Westernization was already developing and at work in Iran. This Shiite tradition of Islam was the predominant branch of the faith in Iran and its emphasis on strict adherence to the Koran, combined with a cult of martyrdom, was to make it a revolutionary force by the end of the 1970s.

THE WHITE REVOLUTION

Securely back in power after 1953, the shah showed that he was a determined modernizer. He proclaimed his so-called "White Revolution" in 1963, and began to transform Iran from a largely peasant society into an urban industrial one, for example, by

attempting to modernize Iran's farms. He believed he was rescuing Iran from centuries of backwardness and propelling it into the front-rank of developed societies. The shah had no patience with his largely illiterate peasant subjects who relied on the teachings of the Koran to guide their daily lives and who regarded the eruption of Western ways in their country with deep suspicion.

DISSENTERS REPRESSED

In the early 1960s, the shah cracked down on Muslim clerics who criticized his rule as

The Ayatollah Khomeini returned to Tehran in 1979, just two weeks after the shah's departure, and established an Islamic Republic.

corrupt and unislamic, driving men like the Ayatollah Khomeini into exile, first to neighbouring Iraq then to distant France. The shah's ferocious secret police, Savak, seemed capable of repressing internal dissent with the routine torture of opponents of the regime, and his oil wealth enabled him to build up a huge army buying the latest American and European weapons.

As his reign continued, the shah became increasingly self-confident and out of touch with his subjects. His ambitions and pretensions eventually became entirely unrealistic. In 1971 he invited ridicule when he staged an elaborate celebration of 2,500 years of imperial Iran because everyone knew his father had been a commoner before he seized power less than 50 years earlier. Worse still in the largely Shiite Muslim society, the shah emphasized Iran's pre-Islamic traditions, even adopting the ancient Zoroastrian religious calendar to link his regime back to the pagan imperial age.

The huge rise in oil prices in 1973, imposed by the oil-producing cartel OPEC, offered the shah even more wealth to fund his dream of a powerful modernized Iran. But the combination of unpopular changes imposed from above and the fantastic corruption of the Iranian elite around the shah lit the fuse of popular discontent below.

CORRUPTION TRIGGERS PROTESTS

A key consequence of the "White Revolution", which brought in new farming techniques requiring fewer men, was that huge numbers of people, especially young men, were driven off their traditional lands into the burgeoning cities. There the contrasts between their poverty or unemployment and the oil-based wealth of the tiny and corrupt Westernized elite was shocking. Despite Iran's natural wealth, the shah's regime refused to respond adequately to the needs of the millions of internal migrants and poor city-dwellers. Instead of cementing his hold on power, the "White Revolution" fuelled a rapidly disintegrating society where corruption and discontent together were spiralling out of control.

By the autumn of 1978, when Western leaders still fawned on him as their regional gendarme for the Gulf, the shah's hold on power was rapidly slipping. Huge street demonstrations across Iran's major cities, involving Muslim clergy, secular radicals, and those made unemployed by the shah's misguided economic policies, were wearing down the security forces and producing near chaos. In a sudden fit of concern about human rights, the United States refused to supply crowd-control equipment like rubber bullets, but the shah's soldiers were unwilling to shoot live ammunition at their fellow Iranians. In fact, the shah seemed to believe his own propaganda that he was the father of his people, and was reluctant to order a bloodbath in order to preserve his own power.

THE SHAH WITHDRAWS

Eventually the shah's own courtiers and US advisers recommended that he withdraw from Iran to calm the situation. They hoped that the generals would be able to control the country once the much-hated shah, had withdrawn. Like some of the shah's non-religious opponents, these advisers still grotesquely underestimated the Ayatollah Khomeini's support in Iran and thought that with the shah gone the opposition would fragment.

US INVOLVEMENT FUELS CRISIS

The shah's humiliating flight "on vacation" ought to have marked the end of his regime. In a way it did, but still millions of Iranians who could remember his comeback in 1953 feared that the United States would somehow engineer his return to power. Ironically, President Carter's orders to the US diplomats and military personnel in Iran to foster good relations with the new regime served only to confirm suspicious minds there that the CIA was hatching a plot to strangle the new-born Islamic Republic.

The shah's exile posed a real dilemma for the American President. If Carter abandoned him to his lonely fate, then other US allies would conclude that Washington could not be relied on in times of adversity, but when Carter agreed to let the ailing ex-shah receive medical treatment in America in October 1979, he triggered an explosion of popular protest in Iran. Students stormed the US embassy in Tehran and the relatively moderate government led by Mehdi Bazargan was toppled.

The 55 US hostages seized in the US embassy became a symbol of American weakness and Iranian radicalism. The ayatollah insisted that Iran "would export our revolution to the whole world." Suddenly the modern world awoke to the threat of a global religious uprising of Islamic fundamentalists. When the Americans bungled an attempt to rescue the hostages in April 1980, the prestige of the Iranian Revolution soared and the radical clerics pressed on with their campaign to outlaw all non-Islamic influences and to turn the clock back. The liberal and Marxist opponents of the shah were now purged as modernizing enemies of Allah just as the shah's own supporters had been.

Although active support for the ayatollah's brand of Islam was limited largely to fellow Shiites, especially in South Lebanon, ultra-conservative Arab monarchies, like those in Saudi Arabia and along the other side of the Persian Gulf, took no chances and clamped down on any sign of religious opposition.

THE EIGHT-YEAR WAR

Iraq's secular dictator, Saddam Hussein, was emboldened by radical Iran's isolation and the apparent turmoil on the streets of Tehran and made plans to seize the oil-rich regions of Iran bordering Iraq. In September 1980, the Iraqi army invaded Iran but instead of leading to the collapse of the Islamic Republic this invasion rallied Iranian nationalists as well as Islamic fundamentalists behind the ayatollah's regime. Mobilizing an ill-equipped army of fundamentalist foot soldiers, backed up by the shah's expensive weaponry bought from the West before 1979, the ayatollah's troops fought Iraq to a standstill. Over the next eight years the two countries waged a bitter war reminiscent of World War I, with its use of mass infantry attacks by Iran and poison gas by Iraq.

PEACE WITH IRAQ

Shortly before his death in 1989, the aging Ayatollah Khomeini agreed to peace with Iraq, though it was "more bitter than poison" to do so. However, his global radicalism was not entirely spent. Khomeini issued a fatwa denouncing the ex-Muslim author Salman Rushdie, for blasphemy in his book *The Satanic Verses*, in effect sentencing him to death. This dramatic attack on freedom of speech confirmed Western antagonism for the values of Khomeini's Islamic Republic.

To be fair, there was more political freedom in Iran than in many of its Arab neighbours. Within a limited spectrum, determined by the ayatollahs, there were multi-candidate elections of a type unknown between Iran and Israel. In 1998, a moderate Islamic Ayatollah Khatami defeated the sitting President Rafsanjani in a remarkable transition of power. Nonetheless, ultimate authority lay with Khomeini's successor, Khamenei, the first president of the Islamic Republic and presiding ayatollah after 1989. Conservative clerics backed by Khamenei did all they could to thwart Khatami's reforms and his friendship with the West.

One of the rulings of the Islamic Republic was that women had to wear the veil. Westernized Iranians were just a few of those who objected to its reintroduction.

Afghanistan 1979–2001

Nothing has challenged the complacency of the western world more than the growth of Islamic fundamentalism since 1979. Even more than the revolution in neighbouring Iran, the success of the Taliban movement in Afghanistan in the mid-1990s demonstrated that a revolution could tackle the western world head on.

Religious ideals instead of secular values were the driving force behind the Taliban's radical attempt to re-establish what they saw as the pure form of original Islam in Afghanistan. Secularised Westerner watched with incomprehension as the new regime stamped out everything they valued, from women's rights and sexual liberation to the television and tape-recorder. Behind the innocent-sounding term 'Taliban', which means 'students', lay the starkest ideological challenge to the triumph of the West at the end of the twentieth century.

THE ORIGINS OF CONFLICT

Afghanistan was one of the few countries around the world to avoid subjection to a European colonial power in the nineteenth century. British attempts to subdue this mountainous land ended in catastrophe in 1842. Yet although this was an early example of how guerrilla warfare could defeat a modern European army, Afghanistan's kings were well aware that modern weapons and technology were good insurance against invasion by the country's imperial neighbours, the British empire in India, Russia in Central Asia and Iran to the west.

The rulers of Afghanistan were also aware that their kingdom was far from a united one. It was a patchwork of different ethnic groups, scattered across its mountainous terrain. The rulers came from the Pashtuns, the largest group but still less than half the population. Persian-speaking Tajiks and Turkic Uzbeks were important in the north and although every Afghan was a Muslim they were divided between the Sunni (which follows the strict saudi or Wahabbi interpretation of Sharia law, drawn mainly from the Pashtun tribe and comprising the majority of the Afghan population), and Shiite (the Iranian-influenced branch of Islam, comprising the Tajik and Hazara minority in Afhgainstan) branches of the faith.

For much of the twentieth century, Afghan kings looked to Turkey as the model of how an Islamic society could modernise its institutions and society in order to survive as

17 July 1973 *King Zahir Shah overthrown by cousin Daud who proclaims Republic*	**24 Dec 1979** *Soviet forces invade Afghanistan*		**May 1986** *Babrak Kamal stays in Soviet Union for "medical treatment", security chief, Mohammed Najibullah becomes President*

1970

27 April 1978 *Communist seize power in coup against President Daud*

27 Dec 1979 *President Amin murdered and replaced by Babrak Kamal*

1985

15 Februar 1989 *Last Soviet troops lea Afghanistan*

High in the mountains of Kunar province in May 1980, Mujahideen "holy warriors" take a rest from their struggle against Soviet intervention in their country.

an independent state. But when the kings made efforts to modernise their country they ran into resistance from deeply conservative tribesmen, especially when they tried to end the confinement of women in 'purdah'. Adult women lived literally 'behind the veil' both at home in their separate quarters curtained off from any visitor, and on the rare occasions they went out when they wore a 'burkah' covering them from head to foot. King Amanullah was overthrown by rural rebels in 1929 when he tried to give women freedom to emerge from 'purdah'.

Male chauvinism and Islamic rigidity seemed to have weakened by 1959 when women were legally permitted to choose whether to wear the veil or not. In the next two decades in cities like the capital, Kabul, Western clothes became more commonplace and education was extended to at least a significant part of the urban population, boys and girls alike. The Afghan government tried to play its position wedged between the Soviet Union and allies of the

25 May 1992 *Fighting between Hikmatyr's forces and Mujahideen in Kabul starts four more years of bitter civil war*

~~ly 1989~~ *Start ~~~ civil war*

4 April 1996 *Mullah Omar, wrapped in cloak of the Prophet, proclaimed Emir of Afghanistan, i.e. spiritual ruler*

20 August 1998 *US airstrikes on Afghanistan in revenge for Al Qaeda bombings of US embassies in Kenya and Tanzania on 7 August, 1998*

9 September 2001 *Arab suicide bombers disguised as journalists murder Shah Massoud*
7 October 2001 *U.S. airstrikes begin*

15 April 1992 *Kabul falls to Mujahideen – Afghanistan proclaimed an "Islamic State"*

October 1994 *First appearance of Taliban fighters in southern Afghanistan - they oppose all other factions*

26 September 1996 *Taliban capture Kabul and lynch former Communist President Najibullah*

April 1997 *Osama Bin Laden comes to Kandahar from Northern Alliance territory*

2000

11 September 2001 *2001 Bin Laden supporters hijack 4 US airliners to attack New York and Washington*

Mid-November 2001 *Taliban forces disintegrate – Kabul falls to US-backed Northern Alliance*

West like Pakistan and Iran, in order to get aid from both superpowers. The Soviets were more successful than the Americans at attracting the support of Afghan modernisers who saw the Soviet Union as the model for a secularised country.

THE SOVIETS INTERVENE

In 1973, the last king of Afghanistan, Zahir Shah, was deposed (while on a state visit to Italy where he remained in exile) by pro-Soviet officers and his own intriguing brother-in-law Daud, who established a secular republic, only to be murdered by his former Communist allies, Nur Taraki and Hafizzulah Amin, in April 1978. (These two also later quarrelled, resulting in Traki's murder by Amin in October 1979). Briefly, pro-Communist forces flouted Muslim tradition and the new regime announced radical social reforms as well as economic changes. But much of the population rejected this sudden departure from ftraditional Islamic ways and the interference with private property and traditional agriculture.

The presence of Soviet advisers and their families also seemed to undermine Afghanistan's proud independence. A savage rebellion in the western city of Herat, lead by an Afghan army officer, Ismail Khan, saw the local Soviet advisers and their families slaughtered after education for women was introduced into the city. Terrible reprisals were launched by Soviet bombers but the new Communist regime was visibly tottering. At Christmas 1979, the Kremlin decided to intervene in Afghanistan to prevent the regime's collapse. The Soviet leaders acted ruthlessly. Although the Soviet troops were ostensibly invited in by President Amin, on their arrival, they murdered Amin and installed a rival Communist regime in his place. The Kremlin regarded Amin as the source of Afghan discontent because he had flouted Islamic tradition and became embroiled in faction fighting within the Afghan Communist party at a time when it was vital to unite against the Mujahideen.

The Kremlin hoped a new leader, Babrak Kamal, would calm the situation, but the occupation of Afghanistan by 100,000 Soviet troops only fuelled resentment. Tribal divisions and the split between Shiites and Sunni Muslims faded away in the face of indignation at foreign occupation.

Afghanistan's terrain and the people's traditions of warfare meant that the Soviet forces and their local allies faced a formidable opponent. Calling themselves soldiers of God or Mujahideen, and appealing to Islam's tradition of 'jihad' or struggle against unbelievers the resistance had a formidable appeal, but adding enormous strength to the Mujahideen guerrillas was the United States itself. The US President Ronald Reagan saw supplying weapons and money to the anti-Soviet Afghans as a way of sapping the strength of the rival superpower which he regarded as an 'evil empire'.

The Mujahideen's use of American anti-aircraft missiles like the shoulder-launched Stinger in the mid-1980s, greatly reduced the ability of the Soviet forces to dominate the battlespace with bombers and helicopters. In addition to human casualties, the Red Army lost 600 aircraft in the 1980s. The war was becoming too costly for the Soviet Union.

When Mikhail Gorbachev became Soviet leader in 1985, he started to look for ways to withdraw from Afghanistan. He backed a new Communist leader there, the ruthless security chief, Najibullah, who tried to repackage himself as a Gorbachev-style reformer without convincing the guerrillas of anything except that the regime was on the run. In February 1989, Gorbachev withdrew the Soviet troops though he continued to back Najibullah's regime with money and weapons, keeping it in precarious control of Kabul. However, once the Communist system collapsed in the Soviet Union itself in December 1991, it was only a matter of waiting for the thaw in the coming spring for the Mujahideen to start a victorious march on Kabul in April, 1992. Abandoned by Moscow and unable to reach the Bagram airbase to fly away, Najibullah and his close relatives took refuge in the UN compound in Kabul. They were safe there, for a while.

THE MUJAHIDEEN TAKE POWER

Meanwhile the West's interest in Afghanistan had waned with the collapse of Communism in the Soviet Union itself. The fall of Kabul to the Mujahideen was hardly noticed by Westerners. However, for Afghans the fall of their Communist regime did not mark an end to conflict. Years of bitter guerrilla warfare had scarred the population. Ancient warrior

traditions had been hardened by the savagery of a conflict which had also bred cynicism and fanaticism in equal measure. To fund the war effort drug smuggling had been vital.

Many ordinary Mujahideen fighters had been brutalised and de-socialised by the conflict. This became clear when the victorious fighters descended on the urban strongholds of the defeated Communist regime like the proverbial wolves among flocks of sheep. The collapse of Najibullah's forces left the people of Kabul defenceless. Many might have been happy to see the Soviet-backed regime out of power, but they anticipated their liberation from it rather differently from the rampage of looting and rape which followed.

Years of bitter fighting in the mountains had turned the young guerrillas into ruthless men loyal only to themselves and their commanders. Now the various Mujahideen leaders showed themselves bent on maximising the profits of victory regardless of the costs to the rest of the population.

Because the guerrilla war had been based on local loyalties and regional identities the warlords soon effectively carved the country into fiefdoms. They saw the capital Kabul merely as a suitable place to wage their power struggle over , access to bribes from international humanitarian aid and the profits of drug smuggling.

During the war up to four million Afghans fled their country, mainly to neighbouring Pakistan. Just as the Palestinian refugee camps around Israel's borders had acted as breeding grounds for radicalism, so the Afghan camps in Pakistan became centres of renewed Islamic fundamentalist influence. The squalid conditions in the camps and the sense of abandonment by the West once the Soviet Union had been defeated produced a generation of bitterly resentful youth in the 1990s, whose religion pronounced a plague on both houses of materialism, the defunct Soviet model but also, and more ominously, on the triumphant American version. In the early 1990s, these students or 'Taliban' returned to Afghanistan to be bitterly disillusioned by the infighting and criminality of key anti-Soviet warlords.

They found a spokesman in a self-taught mullah, Muhammed Omar, who had lost an eye in the struggle against the Russians. In 1994, supported by a handful of students with only 16 guns between them, Mullah Omar took on a local warlord who had kidnapped two girls intending to let his men in a camp near the city of Kandahar rape them. To everyone's surprise the Talibs easily defeated the larger force. Meeting out divine justice, the Mullah had the warlord executed. It was the beginning of a dramatic rise to power.

Although Mullah Omar's grim law-and-order message certainly struck a cord with millions of ordinary Afghans exhausted by fifteen years of civil strife, his group would not have made the rapid progress it did over the next two years without help. Pakistan wanted to restore order in Afghanistan so it could trade with Central Asia via its neighbour. It now stopped the help it had given the various Mujahideen during the 1980s and gave money and guns to the Taliban movement. Rich Saudi fundamentalists were also attracted to the Mullah's reverence for their land as the source of pure Islam.

THE RUTHLESSNESS OF THE TALIBAN

Unlike squabbling Mujahideen leaders who had caused thousands of deaths but spared each other, the Mullah Omar executed captured leader. When they captured Kabul in April 1996, Taliban fighters went to the UN compound and seized Najibullah and his brother from hiding and strung them up. It was a sign that they intended to subdue the whole country, with disregard for international law. The Mullah Omar took the title of Emir, leader of the faithful. By definition, his opponents were damned.

With much of the country under Taliban control, religious edicts issued by the Emir obliged all women to wear the full burka and restricted their education and economic activities to the home. Many war widows faced desperate poverty if they could not work to feed their children. But the Taliban insisted God or their families would provide. Symbols of Westernisation like television and cassette recorders were banned.

Relief at the end of civil war and lawlessness was soon tinged for many with resentment at the religious obligations imposed by the Taliban. However, others were very attracted by this reversion to primitive Islamic values. Many foreign Muslims, especially Arabs and Chechens had come to

Afghanistan to fight the Soviet Union. They saw the country as unpolluted by materialism and a model for other Muslim societies. Among them was the son of a Saudi millionaire, Osama Bin Laden, who had fought with the Mujahideen in the 1980s.

By the mid-1990s, Bin Laden had rejected both his old American sponsors in the war against Communism, and the royal Saudi government. He had become a key figure in the shadowy world of Middle Eastern Islamic activists who denounced capitalism and Communism plus their own Arab

An undated photograph of Osama Bin Laden at an undisclosed location in Afghanistan. He is the chief suspect in the September 11 attacks on New York and Washington.

governments as puppets of America and soft on Israel. Driven out of his base in Sudan for his support of anti-US terrorism, Bin Laden returned to Afghanistan in 1996 wherehe sought out his old comrades from the anti-Soviet struggle, but he was soon disillusioned with them. These enemies of the new Taliban government were still hoping for US backing and were even prepared to deal with their former enemies in Moscow to acquire weapons for their continuing struggle.

Wary of Bin Laden at first, Mullah Omar became impressed by the Saudi refugee's fanatical Islamic values. He even gave a daughter in marriage to Bin Laden and let him set up training camps for his Al-Quaeda (Citadel) group in Afghanistan. The Taliban movement had confined its ambitions to purifying Afghanistan alone, until the Mullah's meeting with Bin Laden. Now the Saudi exile's grandiose ambitions to ignite a worldwide anti-American struggle in the name of Islam had found a home. Soon his network of supporters would strike at American targets culminating on 11th September, 2001, with the most dramatic acts of terrorism in history.

Bin Laden made the Taliban a global phenomenon, and from the West's point of view a pariah. After 11th September 2001, Taliban Afghanistan went from an experiment in fundamentalism in one society to a head-on conflict with the world's most powerful secular society. It was a struggle in which only a true believer would hope to win, or accept the terrible price of failure his people might have to pay.

POPULAR UPRISINGS

Introduction

The crowd in the streets of Paris in July 1789, storming the Bastille prison, or the swarms of people marching through St Petersburg in February 1917, pulling down the double-headed eagles that symbolized the imperial monarchy, or the vast array of peaceful citizens of Prague filling the square mile of Wenceslas Square in November 1989, are the images of popular revolution that fill our minds. Nowadays contemporary prints or photographs have become a montage interlaced with imaginative reconstructions like Abel Gance's films of the French Revolution and Napoleonic era or Eisenstein's film *October 1917*, let alone more recent Hollywood kitsch. History and propaganda have become almost irretrievably interwoven.

HOPE FUELS MASS PROTEST

Why does the revolutionary urge suddenly grip whole cities, indeed sometimes whole societies? At times specific events like acts of police brutality may trigger popular revolutions, but as Leon Trotsky noted "the mere existence of mass privations is not enough to cause an insurrection; if it were, the masses would be always in revolt." What is needed is what Trotsky called "the bankruptcy of the social regime". When this happens and the possibility of an alternative appears, mass demonstrations occur.

Lenin argued that revolutions occur when the old order has lost its way but a new order has not yet emerged to replace it. The

A young Sandanista guerrilla raises a slingshot and pistol in triumph, surrounded by older comrades in the rebel-held town, 30 June 1979, Masaya, Nicaragua.

decay of the old system, including the weakening of loyalty and discipline among its security forces, leaves room for alternatives that can suddenly well up into public demonstrations.

FEATURES OF POPULAR REVOLUTIONS

Poverty alone does not cause unrest, in fact, quite the contrary. A population whose energy is consumed by finding food and other essentials of existence can prove remarkably quiescent in the face of what outside observers regard as intolerable conditions. In the ancient world, Aristotle understood that "It is also in the interests of a tyrant to make his subjects poor, so that… the people are so occupied with their daily tasks that they have no time for plotting [revolution]." Aristotle's classic example of drudgery making for political stability was the construction of the pyramids of Egypt – building projects intended to exhaust popular energy. Of course, Aristotle had not heard about the version in the Hebrew Scriptures in which the Israelites' treatment by Pharaoh's harsh taskmasters stimulated God to find a prophet to lead his chosen people out of slavery. Some writers have seen Moses as the first revolutionary for that reason, but since others question his historicity it might be better to see him as a literary inspiration.

What the story of Moses illuminates is the importance of a new element or person whose presence makes previously accepted oppression suddenly intolerable. Sometimes generations of meek submission are shattered by a particular charismatic individual or an incident that breaks the dam of pent-up resentments.

The sudden collapse of imposing and even threatening regimes is a striking feature of popular revolutions. As Alexis de Tocqueville, the great French historian of revolution, noted in his own observations of the almost bloodless events in Paris in February 1848, "No one overthrew the government. It just allowed itself to fall."

TWO CAUSES OF UPHEAVAL

Tocqueville was a very rare historian because he was also a prophet. In his capacity as a deputy in the French national assembly, before the 1848 revolution, he warned the complacent and unrepresentative majority on 29 January 1848, that "It is said that there is no danger because there is no riot, and that because there is no visible disorder on the surface of society, we are far from revolution." Political scientists as well as active politicians, on numerous occasions throughout history, and as recently as 1989, have shown themselves insensitive to the stirrings beneath the placid surface of societies as different as early industrial France or the Soviet bloc. Tocqueville warned his contemporaries "We are lulling ourselves to sleep over an active volcano."

Tocqueville drew out two key causes of the coming upheaval: one was the growing sense of inequity that the fabulous wealth a few had achieved through the industrial revolution was fostering among the poor majority; the other was the ignoble complacency and corruption of rulers who seemed indifferent to popular feelings as well as incapable of satisfying their grievances.

Across Europe in 1848, and again in much of Central and Eastern Europe in 1989, the old regimes seemed to disappear almost in a puff of smoke at the first sign of large-scale protests. This sudden collapse showed the waning of the old system's legitimacy behind outward conformity. Even the regime's key servants had lost faith in it or were disillusioned by their leaders' incapacity or corruption.

WHY POPULAR REVOLUTIONS FAIL

The failure of popular revolutions lies very often precisely in their spontaneity and the lack of a disciplined political party organizing them. Although the absence of identifiable political leaders makes police repression or the murderous work of death squads more difficult, it also means that at key moments the crowd in the streets or the population at large may lack coordination. By contrast, counter-revolutionary forces, which may have been winded at first by their own rulers' mistakes and the scale and suddenness of popular protest, can fall back on institutions like the army and police to organize a counter-attack.

For instance, in 1848, traditional rulers in Vienna and Berlin bowed to popular pressure to grant constitutions and liberalize their regimes, but by mid-1849 professional armies led by vigorous martinets with no time for liberalism had been able to strike at the revolutionaries, dividing them and conquering them piecemeal. Poorly organized popular militias proved generally inadequate when fighting against regular troops. In Beijing in the spring of 1989 the Chinese communist gerontocracy found loyal troops to fire on student demonstrators and others who had occupied the city centre for months.

Technology, too, tends to side with the forces of repression: the new railways gave armies mobility and the ability to move swiftly against ill-equipped rebels in 1848–9. The new telegraph wires running alongside railways enabled governments, police, and soldiers to communicate across long distances, coordinate their activities, and out-manoeuvre the revolutionaries.

The contrast between the failure of the Russian revolution in 1905 to topple the autocratic imperial system, despite massive demonstrations in the cities and widespread revolt throughout the countryside, and the sudden and complete implosion of the regime in 1917 is striking. A crucial element on both occasions was the response of railway workers: in 1905, they continued to operate the system, allowing loyal troops to travel throughout Russia in order to stifle dissent in one place after another; in 1917 the railway strike compounded the government's crisis and was so successful that Tsar Nicholas II was even late for his own abdication!

The communist leader of Czechoslovakia, Alexander Dubcek, speaks to supporters during the May Day Parade in Prague on 1 May 1968.

WHEN ENTHUSIASM WANES

Ordinary people can only remain mobilized in the streets and at the barricades for so long. After a while they must feed themselves and their families. If they have flooded out onto the streets in protest or triumph, there is always the morning after when mundane concerns return to preoccupy them.

It was the recognition that the tide of popular revolution naturally recedes that led Franz Kafka, who witnessed the fall of the Habsburg monarchy in his native Prague in 1918, to note that afterwards the "slime of bureaucracy" remains. Unless led by clear-eyed ideological activists, the toppling of thrones still leaves layers of state administration to carry on much as before once revolutionary enthusiasm has waned.

INSPIRING HEROIC MYTHS

Failure does not kill faith in revolution as a cure for social ills if the causes remain despite the attempt to change conditions. As an elderly veteran of Emiliano Zapata's crusade in Mexico 50 years before told a visiting journalist in 1964, "I believe that… the next revolution is already written… Since Zapata many have tried but nothing happens. Everything is crushed because God has not given the word yet. Then suddenly we'll see the revolution of the poor against the rich in Mexico. Not now, I don't think, but it will come. I can't say who will be the leader, but it must be someone." And 30 years on, the anonymous masked Sub-Comandante Marcos appeared, leading the Zapatista rebels in the Chiapas Province of southern Mexico. The legacy of failure – not only in Mexico – is not necessarily perpetual resignation and subjugation, but the development of a heroic myth that inspires future generations to tackle their own hardships in a revolutionary fashion, if the hope of real reform is closed off.

Russia 1905

Failed revolutions often teach greater lessons than successful ones. In 1905 Imperial Russia collapsed into chaos as more than a century of grievances with arbitrary government by the autocratic tsars culminated in revolt. The widespread discontent of a new urban industrial working class and the ancient resentments of the peasantry exploded in a spontaneous revolution that briefly looked as though it would overthrow Europe's most powerful and absolute monarchy. Although the tsar repressed insurgents, eventually routing the revolution by the beginning of 1906, the events of 1905 provided an unexpected dress rehearsal for the volatile upheaval of the Russian Revolution of 1917.

REVOLUTIONARY IDEALS INSPIRE MUTINY

From 1825 to 1905, Russia witnessed the development of a uniquely strong and equally unsuccessful revolutionary tradition. Mutinous army officers who were influenced by French revolutionary ideals first challenged the autocratic rule of the Russian emperors in December 1825. They were ruthlessly suppressed but a tradition of conspiratorial activity against the regime

was born. On repeated occasions throughout the 19th century, underground radical groups inspired by revolutionary ideas from the West plotted to overthrow the tsars. The most dramatic moment came in 1881 when Tsar Alexander II was assassinated by a revolutionary. However, bomb attacks like this only redoubled theregime's efforts to repress any dissenters.

A COSTLY WAR FOSTERS DISCONTENT

Throughout the 19th century, radical critics of the tsars failed to motivate mass uprisings. By the beginning of the 20th century, the social and economic conditions in Russia were producing a great deal of popular discontent. In the countryside, the abolition of serfdom had proved a mixed blessing to millions of Russian peasants who were expected to compensate their lords for their new freedom, which was hedged in with all sorts of limitations in any case. As industrial development took off in big cities like the capital St Petersburg or the oil city of Baku, people swarmed off the land to find jobs in factories, hoping to improve their standard of living. But their living conditions were

14 December 1825
Mutiny against Nicholas I

1875–76
The Land and Liberty movement tried to arouse peasant unrest

1850

February 1863
Alexander II decrees emancipation of the serfs in Russia

1870

1 March 1881 *Assassination of Alexander II in St Petersburg*

often squalid and their work unsafe. The tsarist regime allowed no trade unions or representatives, but ordinary people still tended to look to their emperor for reform. The people viewed him affectionately as their "Little Father" and any problems they blamed on his subordinates. It was inconceivable to most of them that the tsar would alow them to suffer in this way if he was properly informed of the full extent of the hardships they were forced to endure.

Although Russia was in most ways backward compared with Western European states, (for example, it had a primitive and ineffecent agricultural system), like many such states it pursued a policy of imperial expansion. In early 1904, Russian ambitions to control Korea collided with Japan's

Officers on duty in front of the Winter Palace on "Bloody Sunday" were overwhelmed by the number of protesters and shot into the crowd, killing at least 200 people.

interest in the country. To the surprise of the overconfident Russians, the Japanese proved much better organized for war and quickly routed the Russian army and navy in the Far East. This came as a tremendous shock to Imperial Russian prestige. Defeat combined with the economic disruption caused by the war sparked the rapid rise of discontent back in European Russia, 8,000 miles west of the war zone.

BLOODY SUNDAY

On 9 January 1905 a huge column of workers and their families, led by a priest, Father

1894
Nicholas II inherits the throne

9 January 1905
"Bloody Sunday" – demonstrators massacred in St Petersburg

1890

February 1904
War with Japan breaks out

October 1905
Nicholas II concedes an elected Parliament, the Duma

1910

George Gapon, wound their way from the industrial suburbs of St Petersburg to the tsar's Winter Palace in the centre of the city. Carrying religious icons and singing hymns, the protesters hoped to appeal to their Little Father to improve living conditions. In fact, Nicholas II was not in the city, but his guards were, and they panicked in the face of the 200,000 demonstrators, and fired into the crowd. "Bloody Sunday", as the day has been remembered in history, ensued. Cossacks scattered the survivors, but at least 200 people died on the square.

The bloodshed destroyed the benign reputation of Nicholas II. The naive and unquestioning loyalty of the vast majority of the population was shattered, as the reality of the event sank in. The radical novelist, Maxim Gorky, immediately saw the

Eisenstein's film, Battleship Potemkin, *commemorates the failed 1905 uprising, focusing on the mutiny on the Potemkin. This scene shows the Odessa steps massacre, where insurrectionist activity had broken out after the body of a mutineer had been laid in state on the shore at Odessa, subsequent to the mutiny. The uprising was brutally crushed by soldiers.*

significance of the atrocity, writing: "Today inaugurates revolution in Russia. The Emperor's prestige will be irrevocably shattered by the shedding of innocent blood."

STRIKES LEAD TO ELECTED ASSEMBLY

Strikes spread like wildfire across Russia. Peasants revolted. Some soldiers and most famously the crew of the cruiser *Potemkin*, on the Black Sea, mutinied, the latter sparked off when rotten meat was brought on board for the crew. The revolt resulted in the death of a sailor, Vakulinchuk, whose body was laid in state on the shore of Odessa. When the people of the city, where insurrectionist activity was also occurring, saw this, further unrest was stirred up, which was violently suppressed by the military in the city. For a brief period it looked as though the Tsarist regime would implode completely.

Faced by a general strike in October 1905 and the emergence of revolutionary self-appointed local governments called soviets in St Petersburg and Moscow, Nicholas II made tactical concessions. He agreed to call an elected assembly, the Duma, which satisfied many of the better-off and educated in Russia who wanted the country to follow the West European model of constitutional government, and feared the growing chaos in the streets and countryside. However, the tsar insisted on keeping his right to rule by decree when a state of emergency existed. The Duma, like the local councils, exercised little real power and soon enjoyed little respect.

THE REBELLION FALTERS

The tsar also made peace with Japan, freeing up troops to deal with Russian dissidents. To Nicholas II's great advantage, his opponents were incredibly disorganized. Even in the big cities little was done to coordinate revolutionary activities between St Petersburg, Moscow, and other highly populated urban centres. Much of the countryside was in turmoil but, without guidance, the peasants looked no further than their own locality, chasing away area landlords or bailiffs.

By contrast the Imperial Army could coordinate repressive measures across the whole of Russia. Loyal troops used the railways to travel from one hot spot to the next. Unimpeded by railway workers who had the power to sabotage their movements but did not, and helped by the continuing operation of the telegraph system, Nicholas II's forces were able to coordinate and mobilize across Russia's vast territory with ease. Savage reprisals against insurgents finally suppressed disorder in 1906.

THE REVOLUTION GOES UNDERGROUND

The revolutionaries learned from the events of 1905, but the tsar did not. Nicholas II failed to realize that suppressing domestic discontent, rather than removing the sources of it, would only continue to jeopardize his hold on power and the loyalty of his people. Instead of trying to build an alliance with the moderate members of the new Duma, the tsar did all he could to sidetrack it and revert to his old ways of ruling without consulting his subjects. Once war broke out again in 1914, the stability of the entire empire would be threatened – but this time by revolutionaries who were better equipped – organizationally and ideologically – to win power.

Mexico 1910–19

The long years of revolutionary upheaval in Mexico after 1910 laid the foundation for the longest-lasting regime of the 20th century. The rule of the Institutionalized Revolutionary Party (PRI) evolved into a corrupt authoritarian system, with most of the faults of the old order it had swept away. The PRI finally lost power in 2000.

SPANISH COLONIAL RULE

The roots of the explosive situation in Mexico in the early 20th century could be traced to the three centuries of Spanish colonial rule begun in 1519, which had shattered the old pre-Columbian civilization, exterminating a huge number of indigenous Indians, and established the rule of a new Spanish elite and a new religion, the Catholic Church. Land distribution remained hugely inequitable, with Mexicans of Indian origins largely disinherited.

The collapse of Spanish rule in 1821 was a by-product of Spain's occupation by Napoleon after 1808 and her inability to recover control of colonies that had learnt to live independently, as well as being due to a Mexican insurgency, but political stability failed to materialize as the victors over Mexico's Spanish rulers fell out among themselves. The new republic succumbed to its first military coup d'état within a year. Another coup 18 months later reversed the results of the previous upheaval. And so it went on for much of the 19th century as regional leaders, generals, and would-be representatives of Mexico's largely poor populace failed to agree on a legitimate political system. Ensuing governments, like that of the first President of Indian heritage, Benito Juárez, provided hopeful but brief interludes of stability. Although thwarting a French attempt to impose a foreign ruler, Juárez, like so many before him, failed to provide any lasting constitutional order.

Later a young hero of the war against the French, Porfirio Diáz, tried to prevent Juárez's re-election and defeated Juárez's successor when he ran again in 1876, on the slogan that no Mexican President should be allowed to be re-elected. Diáz stuck to that principle in 1880 – at least formally – but secretly arranged for a stooge candidate to be elected as his successor. From 1884, however, Diáz abandoned ruling from behind the scenes and manipulated his own re-election in fraudulent polls up to 1910.

January 1876 *Porfirio Diáz seizes power*

20 November 1910 *Francisco Madera denounces election fraud and issues Plan of San Luis Potosi*

21 May 1911 *Diáz agrees to go into exile; Francisco Madera calls fresh elections*

15 October 1911 *Francisco Madera overwhelmingly elected*

1880

21 June 1910 *Diáz re-elected for seventh time*

March 1911 *Pancho Villa and Emiliano Zapata start rebellions in support of Madera*

5 February 1917 *Mexican Constitution no re-election, anti-clerical articles*

18–22 February 1913 *General Huerta seizes power and murders Madera and his brothers*

Diáz's long rule coincided with dramatic economic changes that stimulated the radical transformation of Mexico's still largely rural Indian population. The creation of new railways paved the way for the expansion of mining and steel mills and trade abroad. With petroleum now exportable to North America and Europe for fuel and lighting, Mexico's oil reserves suddenly became a valuable resource.

Diáz recognized that land was the key to his regime's power base and exploited the resources at his disposal. He issued land grants as a way of buying the loyalty of army officers and the local notables of Mexico's provinces. Despite the economic progress of

A group of rebel women and girls, wearing traditional dress, practise their shooting skills for the Mexican Revolution in September 1911.

the country, agriculture remained its main industry and the rapid growth in the peasant population, up 50 per cent during Diáz's rule, made land hunger an ever-bigger issue.

A NATION'S DEBT BONDAGE

Diáz's government defied popular demands for smallholdings and instead encouraged the conversion of common lands into private holdings run by great landlords. These landlords employed peasant labourers in a system of debt bondage. Poor farm workers

10 April 1919 *Murder of Emiliano Zapata*

5 September 1920
Alvaro Obregón elected president

17 July 1928 *Obregón murdered the day after forcing his illegal re-election*

18 March 1938 *President Cárdenas nationalizes the foreign oil companies*

1994 *Outbreak of Zapatista rebellion in Chiapas*

1920

31 July 1926 *Practice of Catholicism "suspended". Cristero rebellion breaks out (lasts until June 1929)*

1946 *PRI established, ruling until election of Vicente Fox in July 2000*

2000

December 2000 *First non-PRI president, Vicente Fox, inaugurated*

20 June 1923 *Pancho Villa murdered*

were forced to purchase all their supplies from stores owned by their landlords on loans advanced at interest against their inadequate pay. Caught in an overwhelming web of debt, the labourers found it impossible to break free. Peasants bitterly resented Diáz's land grants, which drove them off what they regarded as their own common land only to be re-employed to work it under such terrible conditions.

Despite his advancing years, Diáz was determined to stay in power and had not groomed a successor. His system of doling out favours, however, created potential rival centres of power, as local barons emerged in Mexico's regions, controlling the economy and administration, but paying lip-service to Mexico City. After 1907 a sharp economic downturn hit the new industries and in 1909 a young farmer from the south, Emiliano Zapata, demanded radical land reform for the Indian peasants. As the 1910 presidential elections approached, the 80-year-old Diáz ignored the signs of impending social explosion and put his name forward for re-election once again.

DIÁZ CHALLENGED

To his surprise, an effective rival candidate, the rich northern landowner, Francisco Madero, put his name forward and initiated an American-style whistle-stop campaigning train tour, whipping up anti-Diáz enthusiasm. Diáz had Madero arrested, arranged his re-election for a seventh time with the usual landslide majority, and then unwisely released Madero on bail. Madero went to Texas, received assurances of US support, and then returned to Mexico determined to start a rebellion. He issued a call to arms, the "Plan of San Luis Potosi", in November 1910, which not only denounced Diáz's election fraud but proclaimed Madero himself provisional president. Although Madero hadn't explicitly offered to release the Indian peasants from debt bondage, his proclamation inspired revolts in northern Mexico led by Pancho Villa and, in the south, Zapata, promising the poor an end to their grievances.

Faced by rebellion and uncertain of what the US might do, Diáz's generals decided to calm the situation by sending the elderly dictator into exile and inviting Madero to hold elections that he was certain to win. Unimpressed by Madero's compromises with the old guard, within a month of Madero's election as president, Zapata issued his own "Plan de Ayal" in November 1911, demanding the wholesale turnover of land to the indigenous Indians who cultivated it.

In spite of a promising initial platform, in the end Madero failed to satisfy anyone. With mounting unrest in the southern countryside and strikes in Mexico's industrial north, he even antagonized the Americans by taxing the country's increasingly valuable oil production, which was managed by US-owned companies. Madero's military commander, Victoriano Huerta, proved ruthless against peasant and worker protesters, and suddenly turned on his commander-in-chief in February 1913, ordering the brutal murders of Madero and his influential brothers.

Huerta's coup failed to calm the situation. Ambitious Mexican politicians had developed a taste for rebellion, viewing it as the route to power, and refused to accept the general as president without a fight. With Huerta's government colluding with landlords and bosses, ordinary Mexicans also refused to back down as splits in the elite offered a chance of success. Even President Wilson in Washington fostered further upheaval because of a typical mixture of high-minded principle and American self-interest: Huerta had seized power by murder and had no right to rule but he was also offering oil concessions to British not American companies!

President Wilson put US influence behind a rich northern oligarch, Venustiano Carranza, against Huerta. Carranza used the peasant armies of Villa and Zapata, but as soon as victory was in his grasp he turned regular troops on their men and chased the remnants of their forces into remote rebel strongholds. Zapata was tricked into an ambush and murdered in April 1919.

THE 1917 CONSTITUTION

Although Carranza represented powerful economic lobbies, he had one radical policy that offered a real break with the Mexican past. Like many northern Mexicans, he regarded the Catholic Church as superstitious and corrupt and blamed it for keeping the largely peasant Mexico in thrall.

His new constitution in 1917 proclaimed a sharp separation of church and state and signalled the beginning of a bitter battle between the Mexican revolutionaries and the Catholic Church. The constitution also promised land reform and the end of debt bondage as well as the eight-hour day and trade union rights, but getting these clauses honoured was easier said than done.

The only other aspect of the 1917 constitution that had a lasting impact was its ban on any president serving for more than one term in office, a reform long ago promised by Porfirio Diáz, who forgot it once enjoying the fruits of office. The Mexican president was to have great power but only for a limited time. It was the only term in the constitution that has been respected ever since.

Whatever stability gained by Carranza was compromised by his manipulation of the 1920 election. Enraged by such fraud, old enemies, like Pancho Villa and the rancher Alvaro Obregón, united their forces against him. Carranza was murdered while fleeing towards the coast, and Obregón easily won the election after having Villa murdered.

The new order rejected the influence of the traditional Spanish elite and the Catholic Church. It revived a somewhat imaginary and romantic Aztec and Mayan past to give ancient dignity to its new identity.

Obregón's allies were men who had fought or intrigued their way to the top in the previous decade. Although they wanted to declare the end of the Mexican Revolution in November 1920, they were determined to establish a new regime and a modern, dynamic Mexico.

Obregón talked in a revolutionary way about redistributing land and putting Mexico's interest ahead of business but in practice his regime tried to buy off the most recalcitrant members of the peasantry and working class while leaving big business and large estates intact. The worldwide boom of the 1920s and US demand for Mexican oil cushioned a period of stability, but the religious issue and rural discontent almost destroyed the new system.

"CRISTEROS" CHALLENGE REVOLUTION

Obregón and his hand-picked successor provoked trouble by clamping down on the Catholic Church. As modernizers, they saw it as an obstacle to Mexico's progress, but millions of poor peasants found their only solace in religion. By early 1927 large parts of western and central Mexico revolted, as peasants took up the battle cry, "Long live Christ the King!" For two years the "Cristeros" threatened to overthrow the revolution.

Intending to calm the situation, in 1928 Obregón decided to return to the presidency despite the no re-election rule and was promptly murdered the next day. Rather than continue the untenable fight against the church and the fervent Cristeros, the new government backed down over its anticlerical laws.

Compromising with the Catholic Church was just part of a package of reforms that would end the threat of a peasant counter-revolution. After 1934 Lazaro Cárdenas was the last genuine radical to hold office as president. In his six-year rule he successfully pushed through a genuine land reform that gave 44 million hectares to peasants and made cheap loans and machinery available to them.

In 1938, Cárdenas nationalized the foreign oil companies operating in Mexico, hoping to fund his reforms out of their profits. It was a dangerous step. The United States was horrified and its oil companies organized a boycott of Mexican production. Cárdenas's nationalist gesture might have proved ruinous but for the demand for Mexican oil by the Allies during the Second World War.

CORRUPTION PROVOKES REVOLT

For almost 60 years, Cárdenas's successors handed over power to each other every six years. Although other parties existed, in 1946 the main revolutionary movement, renamed the Institutionalized Revolutionary Party (PRI), was entrenched in power, shamelessly manipulating elections. As the PRI became increasingly corrupt, challenges to its rule arose. In the poor south, militants evoking the memory of Zapata rebelled in 1994. Meanwhile in the richer northern states, business and political opponents of PRI gained backing from the US and called for genuine elections and market reforms. In July 2000, the PRI's candidate conceded defeat to the first non-PRI president, Vicente Fox.

At the turn of the 21st century, the question remained whether Mexico had abandoned her revolutionary past. President Fox promised work, land redistribution, and social justice, but also reassured the US that he would open the country ever more to the globalized economy. The Zapatistas became symbols for the emerging anti-globalist movement, giving Mexico's revolutionary tradition a worldwide audience that Zapata or Pancho Villa had never had.

Peasant men lead a political march in 1984 through the streets of Mexico City, carrying a banner depicting Emiliano Zapata, the Mexican revolutionary.

Hungary 1956

Across Eastern Europe the defeat of the Nazi armies in 1944–5 marked only a liberation of sorts. True, Hitler and his henchmen were driven out by the Red Army, but the Soviet troops came bringing a revolution of their own. Even before the end of the war, Stalin had told a visiting Yugoslav communist, "Each man advances his social system as far as his army can reach." In countries like Hungary, whose government had collaborated with Nazi Germany against the Soviet Union, the Soviet troops had all the rights of occupiers after 1945 and Stalin's forces used their powers to foster the seizure of power by the local Communist Party, which emerged from underground resistance to the old regime.

A NEW COMMUNIST HUNGARY

To satisfy former Western Allies, Stalin permitted the semblance of multi-party democracy, but in practice pro-Soviet sympathizers held all key positions in the new government and Stalin's secret police pulled strings from behind the scenes.

Soviet power could not make communism popular in Hungary. Long memories of Russian invasion in 1849, the more recent experience of Bela Kun's regime and the bitterness felt by many Hungarians at the raping and pillaging that accompanied the Red Army's conquest in 1945, meant that in the 1946 general elections the Communist Party lost to the Smallholders, a popular peasant party with over 50 per cent of the vote.

Stalin's representatives set out to destroy the Smallholders and forced non-communist left-wingers, like the Social Democrats, to fuse with the Communist Party, in what a local communist hardliner, later to be prime minister, Matyas Rakosi, chillingly called "salami tactics" – slicing off one opposition group after another.

Slavish obedience to the Soviet model compounded Hungary's legacy of wartime destruction. The economy floundered as investment and unrealistic targets for industry were pursued at the cost of the standard of living.

STALIN DENOUNCED

Stalin died in March 1953 and no single person succeeded him in the Kremlin. The divisions among his successors began to de-stabilize Soviet control. First of all, in June 1953, East German workers revolted against

6 March 1953 *Death of Stalin announced*

23 February 1956 *Khrushchev denounces Stalin at 20th Congress*

6 October 1956 *Funerals of purge victims – 300,000 demonstrate*

24 October 1956 *First workers' council set in Budapest*

1940

1946 *The Communist Party lost to the Smallholders in general elections*

1955 *Formation of Warsaw Pact*

17 July 1956 *Soviet advisers force Rakosi to resign as Party leader*

23 October 1956 *Demonstrators occupy key buildings in Budapest*

the local Stalinist regime and Soviet tanks had to suppress them. The new First Secretary of the Soviet Communist Party, Nikita Khrushchev, used the crisis to justify executing Stalin's much-feared secret police chief, Lavrenty Beria. Signs of such high-level feuding sent ripples across Eastern Europe.

The Kremlin began to back new reformist communist leaders in the satellite states. To strengthen his position at home and abroad, Khrushchev winnowed out hard line communist leaders to promote himself as the patron of a more relaxed style of government.

In February 1956, Khrushchev shocked the communist elite by denouncing Stalin as a tyrant and mass murderer to a secret session of the 20th Congress of the Soviet Communist Party. News of Khrushchev's revelation spread across the Soviet bloc – a shattering blow to the legitimacy of Eastern Europe's loyal Stalinist puppets. Until now they had claimed that as loyal disciples of Stalin, "the leader and teacher of progressive humanity", they had the right to rule. Khrushchev's turnabout was so shocking that the Polish Communist boss, Bierut, dropped dead in Moscow after hearing the speech.

Bitterness and disillusionment with Stalin-style prime minister and communist hardliner Matyas Rakosi provoke Hungarian anti-Soviet protesters to burn his portrait.

A RETURN TO LENIN'S IDEALS

Khrushchev intended to present himself as a good communist returning to Lenin's true path after Stalin's personal dictatorship, but

| **27 October 1956** Formation of a government of national unity | **30 October 1956** Declaration of Soviet Government | **4 November 1956** Soviet forces attack Budapest – Kadar on Soviet radio | **16 June 1989** Nagy reburied with full honours |

| **October 1956** ...s Kadar appointed First ...etary of Communist Party | **29 October 1956** Britain and France invade Egypt – Suez Crisis distracts West | **1 November 1956** Nagy declares Hungary neutral and leaves Warsaw Pact | **6 November 1956** Hungarian resistance crushed | **1960** **16 June 1958** Nagy and other leaders of the revolution executed | **6 July 1989** Death of Janos Kadar |

in Eastern Europe his charges against Stalin initiated the unravelling of communist authority, especially in Hungary.

When reform-minded Polish communists replaced Stalinists in Warsaw, Hungarians began to believe that change in Budapest was possible. On 6 October, the Hungarian communist leadership permitted the funeral of victims of Rakosi and a huge crowd attended. Then it granted a permit to students to demonstrate on 23 October. The crowd swelled and assembled at the statue of a Polish general who had sided with the Hungarians in 1849. While the Communist Party leaders debated what to do, crowds attacked symbols of the regime, like Stalin's statue in Pest. The secret police found itself alone trying to stop the protests as ordinary policemen sympathized with protesters. No one called out the army, perhaps because the communists did not trust it.

AN ANTI-SOVIET REVOLUTION

The crowds called for the moderate rival of Rakosi in the Party leadership, Imre Nagy. Nagy was still unsure of how far things had gone when he began his first impromptu speech to demonstrators with the word "Comrades"; they shouted at him until he appealed to patriotism and the singing of the national anthem. Nagy's reaction symbolized his dilemma – a communist idealist finding himself at the head of an openly anti-Soviet revolution. His ambivalence helped to seal the fate of the revolution and his own life.

Late on 23 October, the Party appointed Imre Nagy as prime minister, but it also called on the Soviet forces in the country to come to the aid of the secret police in suppressing "counter-revolution". However, that seemed to provoke more disorder.

On 24 October, a high-ranking Soviet delegation agreed to accept Nagy as a mediator between the Hungarian people and the Soviet "big brother". They agreed that the Russian soldiers would withdraw and that the moderate Janos Kadar would replace the hardliner Erno Gerö as First Secretary of the Party.

NAGY LEAVES WARSAW PACT

A new government was announced on 27 October, but it was already behind the public mood as crowds tore down the nation's flags and ripped the communist symbol out of its middle. They then waved these new flags as expressions of their anti-communist patriotism. Across Hungary, provisional committees and workers' councils (an ironic translation of the Russian "soviets") took over from local Communist Party officials.

Pushed from below, Nagy announced on 30 October that Hungary was returning to "a system of government based on the democratic cooperation of the coalition parties as they existed in 1945." This break with the Soviet one-party system immediately provoked demands from the streets that Hungary should assert its full independence by leaving the Warsaw Pact and declaring her neutrality.

SOVIET INVASION

The international situation was central to the Soviet leaders' attitude to the Hungarian crisis. They feared that if Hungary broke away from communism and the Warsaw Pact, other East European countries would follow suit and the Kremlin would lose the outer shield of satellite states that the Red Army had won in 1945 and which now provided a buffer against the Americans and their NATO allies in the West.

Although Khrushchev recognized that a Soviet invasion of Hungary would be a public relations disaster, he could not risk losing control of Hungary. Ironically, two NATO states helped to distract attention from the Soviet Union's invasion. At precisely the same time, Britain and France invaded Egypt in the hope of recovering control of the Suez Canal, which had been nationalized by the Egyptian leader Colonel Nasser.

Hungarian jubilation at the withdrawal of the Red Army was premature. It had only gone to the north-eastern city of Debrecen in order to concentrate its forces and launch a massive counter-offensive with the aid of reinforcements from across the border in the Soviet Union. The counter-attack began at dawn on 4 November.

One of the Hungarian Communist Party leaders, Janos Kadar, who had seemed to support Nagy, suddenly disappeared from Budapest only to reappear among the Soviet forces. He "invited" the troops to stop the "counter-revolution" and protect the Hungarian working class, which was in full revolt against the communist system.

NAGY EXECUTED

Nagy was misled by the future Soviet leader and KGB chief, Yuri Andropov, who was the Kremlin's ambassador in Budapest. Andropov was a shrewd and ruthless operative and he played on Nagy's divided loyalties and his desire to avoid unnecessary bloodshed. After the Soviet troops reached Budapest, Nagy took refuge in the Yugoslav embassy but Andropov tricked him into leaving and then had him seized and shipped off to Soviet-controlled Romania for brutal interrogation before he was executed. (His remains were later buried with those of zoo animals in an unmarked grave along with the corpses of other executed leaders of the revolution.)

Kadar asked Khrushchev to let him execute both Rakosi and Nagy, as if killing the unpopular Stalinist would outweigh any discontent at his murder of the popular reformer. Khrushchev was not so cynical. He packed Rakosi off to a grim exile in Uzbekistan.

More than 200,000 Hungarians fled to refuge in the West before Soviet control was completely restored. Kadar ruled for another 32 years. He died in 1989 only weeks after the reburial of Imre Nagy, marking the beginning of the end of communism in Hungary.

The current prime minister of post-communist Hungary, Victor Orban, launched his political career at the reburial ceremony with a speech denouncing the treatment of Nagy and Hungary's fate since 1956.

Cuba 1959

When a small force of guerrillas in ragged uniforms marched into Cuba's capital, Havana, on 2 January 1959, a revolutionary regime was born – one that would remain a thorn in America's flesh for more than four decades and would spawn armies of guerrilla-imitators as far away as Africa and Asia. The 33-year-old leader of the rebel band, Fidel Castro, would become the most famous revolutionary in the world and has kept that title for more than 40 years.

BATISTA'S CORRUPT REGIME

The Cuban revolution had its roots in the six decades since US intervention in 1898, which had ended the bitter war of national liberation against Spanish rule. For many, rule simply passed from the Spanish to the Americans. Only 90 miles (145km) from Florida, Cuba was forced to institutionalize an American right to intervene in the island's affairs in its 1903 constitution. Cuba's one economic asset, her sugar crop, was monopolized by American companies.

Constitutional democracy, established at the behest of the Americans, had disappeared by the 1950s, when Fulgencio Batista, a former army sergeant, came to power by military coup in 1952. His flamboyantly corrupt regime seemed oblivious to the popular hostility aroused by its flirtation with American gangsters who dominated the island's international tourist scene, reducing many Cubans to the status of croupiers and prostitutes. Batista felt secure in his hold on power because the CIA had acted to prevent

Che Guevara was a skilful guerrilla leader and one of Castro's closest and most trusted friends. He served as Cuba's Minister of Industry from 1961 to 1965.

10 December 1898
Cuba declares independence from Spain

28 January 1909 United States withdraws from Cuba

1880

20 May 1902
Spain recognizes Cuba's independence

1940

10 October 1940
Fulgencio Batista elected president (until 1944)

popular revolution in nearby countries like Guatemala in 1954.

Batista's coup in March 1952 led to the cancellation of the presidential elections in which a young lawyer, Fidel Castro, had run as a candidate for the anti-corruption Ortodoxo Party. Castro soon decided that Batista could only be removed by force. On 26 July 1953 with his brother, Raul, and about 200 mainly student activists, Castro organized an attack on the army's Moncada Barracks in Santiago, hoping to spark a general uprising. The attack was a fiasco. Many activists were killed and Castro was captured soon afterwards, but at his trial Castro turned the tables on the prosecution with a dramatic speech in his own defence declaring "History will absolve me".

In an effort to improve his image in America, Batista agreed to amnesty for his political prisoners, including Castro in May 1955. If the dictator thought they would be grateful, Castro soon proved him wrong, announcing as he left Cuba that he intended to return to overthrow the tyrant.

CASTRO AND CHE GUEVARA TEAM UP

In Mexico, Castro teamed up with the radical Argentinian doctor, Ernesto Che Guevara, and at the end of November 1956, along with about 80 other guerrillas, they embarked in the small boat, *Granma*, in a hazardous journey leading back to Cuba.

Initially Batista regarded Castro's group as little more than a nuisance as it set up base in the mountains 500 miles (810km) east of Havana. However, Batista's troops proved unable to hunt down the guerrillas; they had never had to fight such a determined and fearless enemy. Castro's men were dedicated, in sharp contrast to the government soldiers. Local people resented the army as agents of Batista's regime and refused to provide information on guerrilla movements.

Castro turned out to be a quick learner when it came to organizing a rural resistance movement, as well as a gifted propagandist via radio. In the cities far from his mountain hideouts, people heard Castro's messages, rebroadcast from Florida and Venezuela, undermining both government claims about the fighting and its troops' morale.

Havana's high-rise hotels and fleets of gas-guzzling cars gave the impression that Cuba was prosperous in the 1950s. In spite of progress and declining mortality rates, most Cubans relied on the sugar harvest for their annual income; even in good years many Cubans had no work for half the year.

Unable to galvanize his troops to fight and rejected by a sullen population who despised his corruption, Batista's watched his regime crumble with dramatic suddenness in late 1958 after two years of clashes in the remote mountains of the Sierra Maestra. While

---

10 March 1952 *Batista seizes power*

2 December 1956 *Castro brothers return to Cuba with Che Guevara*

7 February 1959 *Castro proclaims socialist republic*

22–28 October 1962 *Cuban Missile Crisis*

April 1980 *Mariel Crisis: First wave of mass emigration since revolution*

26 July 1953 *Castro's guerrillas attack Moncada Barracks, Santiago*

2 January 1959 *Castro's forces march to Havanna*

15 April 1961 *Bay of Pigs fiasco*

2000

25 November 1999 – 28 June 2000 *Elian Gonzalez Affair*

1 January 1959 *Batista flees to Dominican Republic*

American gangsters held New Year's Eve parties at their night clubs in Havana, at a reception Batista told his generals and ministers that he was leaving in two hours and they could join him. Such was the panic that many came with their wives and mistresses who were still dressed in party frocks. Many wealthy Cubans also fled at this time, settling in Florida, where they became vocal anti-Castro activists.

CASTRO NAMED NEW LEADER

The ignominious collapse of the Batista regime left a brief power vacuum as Castro's men marched to the capital from the mountains. A provisional president and prime minister were sworn in as the old constitution was restored, but it was clear that Fidel Castro held the real power under the title "Maximum leader" and that he enjoyed massive popularity. Soon he assumed formal political power as head of state.

CUBA SHIFTS TO THE LEFT

Few of the hundreds of thousands of Cubans who cheered Castro's arrival in Havana had any clear idea of what his intentions were. Although in later years Castro insisted that he had always been a Marxist, his revolutionary propaganda during the war against Batista only vaguely promised land reform and anti-corruption measures.

The carnival atmosphere in Havana in January 1959 was tarnished by a wave of savage reprisals against Batista supporters who had not fled with him. Castro insisted that the world, not least the Americans, had turned a blind eye to Batista's tortures and murders so it was hypocritical for others to condemn them for settling old scores now. In any case, he added, "The executions were useful, a lesson for the future." There would be no turning back, in other words.

Along with Che Guevara, Castro pushed Cuba more and more in the direction of the Soviet model and into alliance with the Kremlin. Alarmed by the radical leftward shift in Cuba, in 1960 the US Congress cut back the amount of sugar American companies could import from Cuba. In return Castro nationalized American assets in Cuba and turned to the Soviet Union for economic aid.

BAY OF PIGS INVASION

Determined to stop Moscow establishing a missile base so close to the US, and listening to Batista's ex-lieutenants, who claimed that Castro was massively unpopular, the CIA organized a motley invasion force of Cuban exiles hoping to topple Castro. However, the US military was not officially involved in the operation, so neither US airforce nor US navy provided support to the invaders, who landed at the Bay of Pigs in southern Cuba. Castro's troops were highly motivated and by now had Soviet T54 tanks and aircraft to isolate and pound the invaders, who quickly collapsed once American aid, which had been promised by America's president, Kennedy, failed to materialize.

CUBAN MISSILE CRISIS

The fiasco of the Bay of Pigs gave Castro a propaganda coup. It enabled him to discredit any opposition as CIA-inspired, but also led him into a dangerously close alliance with the Soviet Union. Castro agreed to let the Soviet Union deploy nuclear missiles that were targeted at America from Cuba. When the American government discovered this in 1962, it reacted with predictable fury but also adopted a shrewd policy of using its vast naval power to quarantine Cuba and cut it off from Soviet aid and supplies of missiles. For six anxious days in October 1962, it looked as though a global nuclear war might break out as President Kennedy challenged the Soviet leader, Khrushchev, to defy his blockade. At the last minute, the Kremlin backed down without consulting Castro, though it did extract a promise from the Americans to invade Cuba only after Russia withdrew its missiles.

During a government visit to his communist ally, East Germany, on 17 June 1972, the Cuban Marxist leader, Fidel Castro, makes a speech.

CASTRO BACKS GUERRILLA UPRISINGS

After 1962, increasingly Cuba exchanged dependency on America for reliance on Soviet aid. While the economy was nationalized and the country took on many of the traits of a Soviet society, Castro and Che Guevara had not renounced their vision of themselves as models for a new revolutionary wave in the Third World. Che's attempts to ignite similar guerrilla uprisings in the Congo in the mid-1960s and then in Bolivia in 1967 ended in disaster when he was captured and murdered by the cruel and highly efficient Bolivian Army.

Deciding to back other Marxist-Leninist revolutionaries in the 1970s and seeing that his own example was not enough, Castro sent thousands of troops to back new allies fighting counter-revolutionaries. For 15 years, Cuba suffered heavy casualties while fighting insurgents in Angola. But internal struggles surfaced and in 1989 General Ochoa, who led Cuban troops in Angola, was tried and shot, allegedly for corruption but probably for plotting against Castro due to disagreements over the war in Angola.

This painting entitled Love, Justice and Freedom *shows the rescue of Elian Gonzalez at sea and was hung in Little Havana shortly before Elian was reunited with his father.*

ECONOMIC STAGNATION

In the early 1980s Castro's regime faced the first open defiance since the revolution. Decades of economic stagnation frustrated many Cubans and in April 1980, foreign embassies in Havana suddenly found themselves invaded by asylum seekers. One bus even crashed through a guard cordon into the Peruvian embassy. Castro reacted by withdrawing the guards outside embassies, thinking that foreign diplomats would soon tire of their uninvited guests. News of the police withdrawal spread and soon 10,000 Cubans climbed into the embassies. Unlike his ally, East Germany, which faced a similar crisis in 1989, Castro surmounted the challenge by briefly opening the floodgates to emigration and taking the opportunity to expel many Cuban criminals. On 18 April Castro told the exile community in Miami that it could bring its boats to the port of Mariel and pick up any Cubans who wanted to leave the country.

Letting the disgruntled leave was Castro's way of releasing some of the frustrations that had built up during decades when ordinary Cubans were made poorer by ill-thought out Soviet-style policies and an American trade embargo begun in 1960. The collapse of the Soviet Union in 1991 marked the end of Soviet subsidies to Cuba. Demand for the sugar harvest fell dramatically and Castro had to pay for oil imports. Briefly it looked as though Cuban communism might go the same way as the Soviet model. Castro's personal prestige may have been battered by time but his residual charisma as the guerrilla hero who had defied the Yankee giant still sustained his regime more than 40 years on, as did his ruthlessness towards opponents. He also showed willing to abandon his hostility to capitalism and exploit Cuba's climate and beaches for mass tourism, which had disappeared with the fall of Batista. Tourist dollars became his regime's lifeline after 1991.

CUBANS EMIGRATE TO AMERICA

Castro also tacitly let disaffected Cubans flee to Florida in makeshift boats. At the end of 1999, the continuing exodus of Cubans hit the headlines again when the six-year-old boy, Elian Gonzalez, was rescued by the US coastguard floating on a tyre after his mother had been drowned on the crossing to Florida. The boy's father demanded his son's return to Cuba where Castro organized a vast campaign of demonstrations and petitions denouncing the "kidnapping" of the child by his cousins who lived in Miami. After months of wrangling, the US authorities eventually refused the Florida relatives' claim to the child and let his father come to the United States to take Elian back to Cuba. The apparently voluntary return of Elian and his father from America was a propaganda triumph for Castro, who had risked the father's defection to get the child brought back to Cuba. Even in old age and with his regime more isolated than ever, Castro was still able to defy the superpower to the north.

Prague 1968

Alexander Dubcek's doomed attempt to reform communism from within in Czechoslovakia in 1968 was not the failure it seemed after Soviet troops swarmed into the country in August 1968. In 1987, Mikhail Gorbachev admitted that his liberalizing policies of glasnost and perestroika in the Soviet Union owed a great deal to Dubcek's "socialism with a human face". When asked in 1987 what the difference was between the Prague Spring and his own reforms, Gorbachev replied, "Nineteen years."

Unlike East European countries overrun by the Red Army as it advanced on Berlin at the end of World War II, Czechoslovakia did not have a long history of anti-Russian sentiment. Czechs saw Germans as their historical oppressors, something reinforced by Nazi occupation. The fact that Britain and France had abandoned Czechoslovakia to Hitler at the Munich Conference in 1938 also meant that sympathy for the West was probably weaker in Czechoslovakia after 1945 than anywhere else in the emerging Soviet bloc.

Certainly in the post-war elections, the Communist Party scored by far its largest vote anywhere, though at 38 per cent it was still well short of an absolute majority.

AN ESTABLISHED COMMUNIST PARTY

Using its strength in the trade unions and the fact that immediately after the war communists had been placed in key posts both in the police and army, the Czechoslovak Communist Party was able to establish itself firmly in power by the end of February 1948, as the Western-style democratic parties just collapsed.

The ease with which communism was established did not prevent Czechoslovakia from suffering a particularly savage set of show trials in the early 1950s as the local Stalinists rooted out all real and imaginary opposition. Unlike Poland and Hungary, Czechoslovakia did not experience any upheaval in 1956. The country seemed placidly pro-Soviet well into the 1960s. Only fringe cultural phenomena, like absurdist plays by the young Vaclav Havel or films by Milos Forman, suggested any kind of ferment of new ideas, breaking the ice of Stalinist conformity since 1948.

DUBCEK'S UNEXPECTED REFORMS

When the long-serving Communist Party leader, Antonin Novotny, was eased out of

1944 Dubcek returns to Slovakia after working as an interpreter for the Red Army

March 1948 Non-communist foreign minister, Jan Masaryk, dies under suspicious circumstances

1962 Removal of Stalin's statue overlooking Prague.

February 1948 Czechoslovak Communist Party firmly established

March 1953 Death of Clement Gottwald, Stalinist leader

1955

Alexander Dubcek with President Ludvik Svoboda, Oldrich Cernik, and the chief supporter of the Soviet invasion, Vasil Bilak, on 3 August 1968, a few weeks before the invasion.

dissatisfied with the Soviet way of doing things. He felt that this had led Czechoslovakia into economic stagnation, and to fall far behind German or Austrian standards of living, which it had once equalled in the 1930s.

In many ways, Dubcek and his comrades proposed reforms that anticipated what Mikhail Gorbachev tried to achieve in the Soviet Union 20 years later. They hoped that by unleashing enthusiasm for communism instead of keeping the population in a straitjacket of rigid conformity, the economy would rebound, prospering once again.

COMMUNIST ENTHUSIASM SURGES

his job in January 1968, few suspected that his replacement by the unassuming Slovak communist, Alexander Dubcek, would be the catalyst for dramatic change.

To the Soviet leader, Leonid Brezhnev, Dubcek seemed a reliable choice to replace the aged Novotny. After all, hadn't Dubcek spent his formative years living in the Soviet Union, where his idealistic left-wing father worked as an engineer for almost 20 years? Dubcek had only recently returned to his native Slovakia, working as an interpreter with the advancing Red Army, in 1944.

Certainly, Dubcek was committed to a socialist economic system but despite his personal affection for Russia, he was very

Quite soon after Dubcek took charge, ordinary people sensed the regime was relaxing its hold on everyday life. The May Day parade in 1968 was the first to express spontaneous support for Party leaders since 1948. Instead of regimented columns with officially prepared slogans, many workers and their families carried home-made banners and Dubcek was greeted with enthusiasm.

By mid-July, Prague's Warsaw Pact allies were voicing threatening concern about Dubcek's path. The abolition of censorship and the discussion in the press of Soviet crimes, including the question of how their last non-communist foreign minister, Jan Masaryk, fell to his death in March 1948, touched on taboos that Moscow wanted left alone.

6 April 1968 *Communist Party adopts reform-minded action programme*

4 January 1968 *Alexander Dubcek elected first secretary of Czechoslovak Communist Party*

21 August 1968 *Soviet forces occupy Czechoslovakia and arrest Communist Party leaders*

26 August 1968 *Dubcek returns from Moscow*

1965

23 March 1968 *First warning from Warsaw Pact leaders to Dubcek not to tolerate pluralism*

27 June 1968 *"2,000 Words" opposition document published*

22 August 1968 *Congress calls general strike*

June 1970 *Dubcek expelled from Party, demoted to forestry official*

Popular opinion in Czechoslovakia was running ahead of what the Soviet leaders could accept, or what even Dubcek felt was wise. Heady with the relaxation of restraints, people were calling for multi-party democracy. Dubcek admitted to the young playwright Vaclav Havel that he was not sure that free elections would return a communist majority. Soviet ideologues like Mikhail Suslov were concerned that once free elections had been held, even if the communists won the first set, no one could predict the outcome of future elections. Dubcek's style of government provided no guarantees.

At the end of July, Brezhnev confronted Dubcek and demanded that he crack down on anti-communist agitation. Dubcek failed to see how serious the situation was, even when he met the Hungarian leader Janos Kadar on 15 August 1968 and Kadar asked him, "Don't you know what sort of people you're dealing with?" Two other communist leaders visited Prague. The Yugoslav leader, Tito (Josip Broz), also warned Dubcek to back down. Only the Romanian leader, Nicolae Ceausescu, showed any support, but advised Dubcek to take control of internal dissent.

By summoning a Party congress that would decide on new Party rules, including permitting ordinary communists to hold their own opinions at variance with the

Vast crowds of Czechs and Slovaks swarm the streets, protesting at the unexpected Soviet invasion and seizure of power in 1968.

Politburo's, Dubcek set a deadline for pushing Czechoslovakia from a one-party communist state to pluralism. The Kremlin was determined to stop that insidious development, which might give ideas to other Party leaders and threaten the stability of the whole Soviet bloc.

PROTEST AGAINST SOVIET INVASION

On the night of 20 August, the Kremlin coordinated a stealthy seizure of power. Soviet paratroops occupied the Communist Party headquarters in Prague. Helped by local secret policemen, they seized Dubcek and Party leaders even before the rest of the country was aware that it was being invaded, and took them to the Soviet Union.

The Soviets failed to find a Kadar-style puppet at once. President Svoboda refused to dismiss the government and, to the astonishment of the occupying forces, the Czechoslovak Communist Party congress was brought forward from 9 September and held in their presence in Prague. It was a massive vote of defiance by the country's communists. Meanwhile, vast crowds of ordinary Czechs and Slovaks protested in the streets of Prague and Bratislava against the invasion. Speaking the Russian taught at school, they taunted the Soviet troops, who had been told that the CIA had organized reactionaries to seize power in the country.

Meanwhile the Czechoslovak leaders arrived in Moscow in handcuffs. Brezhnev asked in mock distress, "Sasha, what are you doing in chains?" Dubcek's tragic ambivalence about the Soviet Union and his desire to avoid bloodshed played into the Kremlin's hands. Instead of defying Brezhnev, who could not yet find enough willing puppets to fill a new pro-Soviet regime, resignedly Dubcek agreed to return to Prague to re-establish a situation that was acceptable to the Kremlin without abandoning all of his own hopes for reform.

DECLARATION TURNS CLOCK BACK

In fact, by signing the Moscow Declaration with Brezhnev, Dubcek betrayed his reform-minded communists and demoralized the passive resistance at home. His acquiescence laid the way open to the sacking of many of his reformist advisers and even spelled doom for himself in April 1969. Dubcek was then expelled from the Party a year later and turned into an "un-person" for the next 19 years – his name and picture were censored from books and newspapers – working as a forestry official in a remote region of Slovakia.

The so-called "normalization" after 1968 saw more than 600,000 people sacked from their jobs and expelled from the Communist Party. More than ever, the communist regime was one of narrow-minded conformity. As 130,000 mainly better-educated people emigrated and many others were reduced to menial jobs, the economy stagnated for the next 20 years. Although there was a small group of dissidents – ex-reform communists, Catholics, and intellectuals – their voices failed to bring about change. Czechoslovak society slumped into depression after the brief and promising flourishing of the Prague Spring.

Central America 1970s

While Washington denounced the Soviet Union after 1945 for keeping Eastern Europe under control, the United States had its own swathe of puppet states in Central America. For most of the post-1945 era, Washington preferred reliable anti-communist regimes to democratic or popular governments that might flirt with economic policies hostile to the interests of big US corporations in the region. The classic example was the CIA-sponsored coup to overthrow Guatemalan president, Guzman Arbenz, in 1954 when his land reforms threatened the United Fruit Company's holdings.

A TEST-BED FOR DEMOCRACY

Disillusioned with much of US covert foreign policy in the wake of Watergate, Americans elected Jimmy Carter president in 1976, setting a new tone in Washington. Carter emphasized human rights as a key issue in American policy and recognized that anti-Soviet rhetoric would be implausible if the US continued subsidizing dictatorships in the Western hemisphere.

El Salvador became a test-bed for Carter's attempt to mix human rights and promote democracy with pro-American outcomes. In 1979 he pressed El Salvador's military regime to become democratic. Home to more than two million people and with one of the highest birth rates in the world, just 15 families monopolized the economy and held much of the land. Given these inequalities, the existing regime already faced a rural guerrilla movement, the Farabundo Marti Liberation Front (FMLN). Led by intellectuals educated in the Marxist critique of Latin America's neo-colonial dependence on the United States, the guerrillas admired the Cuban alternative of self-reliance and nationalization of previously US-owned businesses.

In a period of democracy in 1972, Christian Democrat leader Napoleon Duarte was elected president but soon overthrown by the military who felt his moderate land reform proposals threatened the dominance of their patrons, the aforementioned Fifteen Families. Duarte was imprisoned and savagely tortured, but survived to later run for re-election.

This brutal coup led to a split in the Christian Democrats, with one section, led by Duarte, hoping that the US would back reform, and a radical wing joining the growing guerrilla movement outside the capital. The split also reflected how the Catholic Church was being radicalized in Central America by

1934 *Augusto Sandino murdered by Anastasio Somoza Sr*

1956 *Anastasio Somoza Sr assassinated*

20 June 1979 *Somoza's guard shoots ABC correspondent, Bob Stewart*

1909–33 *US troops occupy Nicaragua*

1950

1954 *CIA-sponsored coup overthrows Guatemalan president, Albeniz*

1970

23 August 1978 *Sandinistas hold Somoza's parliament hostage*

A Salvadorean Catholic meditates on a mural depicting the assassination of Archbishop Oscar Romero, who was shot while celebrating Mass on 24 March 1980.

decades of oppression and poverty. The Archbishop of San Salvador, Oscar Romero, criticized the death squads organized by the military to silence its critics. On 24 March 1980, he was shot at his cathedral altar while saying a requiem mass for the victims of the death squads.

REPRESSION BREEDS RESISTANCE

The resistance provoked by the coup compounded El Salvador's worsening economic position. The gross national product fell by a quarter between 1979 and 1985 and unemployment rose to 40 per cent.

Although Washington eventually forced the military to accept Duarte as president, his control was vestigial. The war against the FMLN was conducted by the military, who sponsored death squads drawn from their own ranks, and US military assistance and

28 March 1982 *Right-wing ARENA party wins El Salvador elections*

24 March 1980 *Archbishop Oscar Romero murdered*

5 November 1984 *Daniel Ortega elected president of Nicaragua*

11 November 1989 *Last FMLN offensive in El Salvador fails*

19 July 1979 *Sandinistas capture Managua after Somoza flees*

17 September 1980 *Anastasio Somoza assassinated in exile in Paraguay*

1990

25 February 1990 *Violetta Chamorro elected president of Nicaragua*

advisers helped to plan and coordinate the campaign. Washington played down the civilian casualties involved and turned a blind eye to the daily death toll of unarmed suspects shot, which even included foreign priests and nuns, who were suspected of supporting so-called liberation theology.

In March 1982 the US ordered elections to be held, which the FMLN boycotted, to provide legitimacy for the regime. To Washington's horror, its favoured candidates, Duarte's supporters, were beaten by the right-wing ARENA party of deat-squad chief, Roberto D'Aubisson, who had a paramilitary presence in polling places to ensure the right result. In 1984 the US left nothing to chance, ensuring that the "moderate" Duarte won the elections. Even right-wing Republican senator, Jesse Helms, complained that the vote had been "rigged."

SAVAGE MILITARY BACKLASH

The disparity between the resources available to El Salvador's government and the trickle of aid to the guerrillas from the declining Soviet bloc meant that the FMLN could not erode the regime. An offensive in San Salvador on 11 November 1989 led to a savage military backlash and the FMLN leaders decided that negotiating a transition to democracy with their participation offered more hope of positive change than continuing warfare, which left more than 20,000 dead.

The United States' vast resources had enabled it to foil popular discontent in El Salvador and to contain it within a formal democratic framework, although in reality much of the power and wealth remained in the same hands as it had when the crisis began in the late 1970s. In Nicaragua, however, the situation spiralled out of control and threatened Washington with the ugly choice of accepting a Marxist regime that came into power in July 1979, or resorting to force and subterfuge to remove it.

CORRUPTION INSPIRES REVOLT

Nicaragua was a strategically valuable country with a long history of US involvement due to its proximity to the US-controlled Panama Canal. In the 1980s the Reagan administration was determined to prevent any pro-Soviet and Cuban regime coming near that vital asset.

US troops occupied Nicaragua from 1909 until 1933 and restored democracy on their departure, but in practice they handed power over to the leader of the bogus National Liberal Party, Anastasio Somoza Sr, who ruled as a corrupt dictator. After his assassination in 1956, power passed to his sons. US president Franklin Roosevelt infamously described Somoza as "a son of a bitch. But he's our son of a bitch", which remained Washington's attitude until 1979.

From the start, the Somoza dynasty faced opposition by those who resented US domination and the social inequalities that it preserved. The Sandinista guerrillas overthrew the dynasty in 1979, taking their name from the guerrilla chief, Augusto Sandino, who fought the US Marines occupying Nicaragua in the 1920s and was murdered by Somoza in 1934. A Sandino veteran was the father of Daniel Ortega (born 11 November 1945) who became a guerrilla in the fledgling Sandinista movement against Somoza's son in 1963.

Anastasio Somoza Jr plundered the generous foreign aid that was sent to reconstruct Managua after a devastating earthquake in 1972. Also, his regime exported so much blood plasma from Nicaragua that the small country provided 15 per cent of the world's production: a huge proportion for a small country with a poor health service, but very profitable for Somoza. He had amassed a personal fortune of about $100 million by the time of his fall from power and left a country with a foreign debt of more than $1.5 billion, and with much of its industry shattered by his fight to keep power, as his planes bombed factories and the National Guard looted and destroyed assets as they retreated.

Somoza's complete lack of legitimacy was revealed by the inability of his 8,000-strong National Guard, with its sophisticated American weaponry, to defeat the guerrilla insurgency that began in 1978. There were no more than 2,500 Sandinista guerrillas fighting Somoza's National Guard, but they enjoyed vast public support since Somoza was bitterly unpopular. Somoza's National Guard fought a savage war to defend his regime over the winter of 1978–9, and the dictator used his air force to bomb rebel-controlled towns and even parts of the capital, Managua.

Assassination of critics like the newspaper proprietor, Pedro Chamorro, and a US TV journalist in June 1979 shocked the US and convinced Jimmy Carter to abandon Somoza.

SANDINISTAS TOPPLE REGIME

As in other revolutions, the Sandinistas were to discover it was easier to unite people against an unpopular regime than to keep them united behind a new set of policies that inevitably benefited some but not others. Many small businessmen and proprietors had resented Somoza and his cronies for their corrupt extortions but did not want to see private property replaced by socialism. However, many Sandinistas had not spent years in the jungle or prison (such as Daniel Ortega, for instance, who had spent seven years in one of Somoza's grim prisons) only to renounce their dreams of a complete revolution in Nicaraguan society on the downfall of the dictatorship. The Sandinistas feared that the people left to decide would opt for a quiet life once Somoza had fallen rather than make more sacrifices to transform their country into a completely new type of society.

In Russia, workers welcomed the Bolshevik seizure of power in their factories by deciding to increase pay and cut working hours. Similarly in Nicaragua after the collapse of Somoza's regime, productivity fell as workers voted for better conditions. Unlike Lenin, the Sandinistas did not resort to coercive measures to restore output. In spite of their victory over a corrupt dictator, long-term inflationary effects and shortages took their toll on the regime's popularity.

THE CONTRAS' COUNTER-REVOLUTION

Although the Sandinistas had promised free elections, in 1980 they suspended them, largely to avoid revealing splits in their own ranks. The decision made the new junta appear as undemocratic as Castro had after he abandoned multi-party elections upon seizing power in Cuba. Failure to hold early elections helped the Reagan administration to justify its backing for the emerging Contra movement against the Sandinistas.

The Contras were a mixed bag. Some, like Eden Pastora, had been anti-Somoza guerrillas who had fallen out with the Sandinista leaders, but others were former National Guardsmen, who left Nicaragua after the revolution. Although the anti-Somoza veterans were prominent in Western propaganda, former Somoza supporters became the real leaders of the movement, acting as intermediaries for US aid, advice, and orders. The CIA organized the mining of Nicaraguan harbours to damage the economy and frustrate Soviet bloc supplies, and the US defied the World Court in The Hague when it ruled the action illegal and ordered the Americans to pay compensation.

US IRAN-CONTRA SCANDAL

The Iran-Contra scandal that broke in November 1986 threatened to stop US aid to the Contras when the press revealed that the Reagan administration had tried to circumvent congressional restrictions on military aid to the Contras. Reagan officials had set up a complicated scheme to provide money and munitions to the Contras via a deal with Iran, which would also release some Americans held hostage in Lebanon. The US establishment had no stomach for a second Watergate and the Iran-Contra scandal subsided without the Contras losing any aid despite laws passed by congress.

The 1989 election of Reagan's vice-president, George Bush, who had coordinated US policy towards Central America, was bad news for the Sandinistas, especially as the Soviet Union was rapidly waning in the late 1980s and its new leader, Mikhail Gorbachev, was no longer willing or able to subsidize remote allies like Nicaragua.

ELECTIONS END WAR

Daniel Ortega, whose election as president in 1984 had been called into question by a boycott of the election by pro-US candidates, was anxious to end the Contra war, which cost about 30,000 lives, and was convinced of the Sandinistas' underlying popularity despite the hardships of civil war. Thus, he decided to hold presidential elections in February 1990, which would make it difficult for Washington to continue to back the rebels.

Ortega misjudged popular sentiment. Two groups coalesced to swamp his bid for democratic legitimacy. First, there were the US-funded opposition parties backing the newspaper proprietor, Violetta Chamorro, whose husband was murdered by Somoza. Second, many Nicaraguans were sick and tired of war, shortages, and hyperinflation, which had skyrocketed to 13,000 per cent before the elections. Voting for Chamorro offered the clearest way out of the US embargo and the war with the Contras.

Ortega's vice-president, Sergio Ramirez, admitted that the Sandinistas had failed to convince many peasants of the benefits of their policies: "That is why the counter-revolutionary war gradually became a peasant war, dividing the peasants into those who understood the [Sandinista] revolution and those who could not be reached by it."

ERASING THE REVOLUTION

Throughout the 1990s there was a campaign to reverse the Sandinistas' changes and to destroy their memory by, for example, erasing murals depicting their time in power. Even land reforms were reversed to remove the social basis of a pro-Sandinista peasantry.

Many of the socio-economic problems that fostered the guerrilla movements remain unresolved today. High birth rates and poverty convince hundreds of thousands of Central Americans to migrate to the US each year, an index of misery and discontent.

Sandinistas celebrate in Managua, 20 July 1979, after entering the city and overthrowing the corrupt dictator Anastasio Somoza.

EAST GERMANY

The Iron Curtain dividing Germany after 1949, and particularly the Berlin Wall erected in August 1961, starkly symbolized the failure of communism in Europe to achieve its ambitions as a beacon of hope for mankind. Instead of attracting admirers, in the second half of the 20th century communist states had to erect barriers to emigration to keep their own people from defecting to capitalist societies.

After Stalin abandoned hope of a communist-run united Germany in the late 1940s, the Soviet Union promoted a model communist regime in its zone of Germany based in East Berlin, hoping the country would be a vanguard in ideological and economic competition with the West.

By the 1980s, the Soviet economic model failed to achieve the kind of living standards taken for granted even by the poor in Western Europe. Already in 1961, Honecker supervised the building of the Berlin Wall to seal off any escape routes for refugees from Germany. But television knew no boundaries and most East Germans could watch West German TV by the 1980s. Although its adverts exaggerated Western wealth, it was clear that in the economic competition West Germany had won hands down and without sacrificing freedom.

As long as the Soviet Union used force to suppress rebellion, as it did in East Germany in 1953, a sense of hopelessness blanketed not just East Germany but the whole Soviet bloc. However, the emergence of Mikhail Gorbachev in March 1985, the first fit and youthful Soviet leader for a generation, began to loosen the hold of despair.

While the aging East European leaders kept their states in the grip of "normalization" Gorbachev initiated a policy of "openness" (glasnost) in the Soviet Union and talked about the system's need for reform (perestroika). Almost 20 years on Gorbachev was recognizing the same socio-economic logjam that one-party control exerted over Soviet-type societies, just as Dubcek did in Czechoslovakia. In the mid-1980s, Gorbachev brought Dubcek's critique of how a previously revolutionary Communist Party had become moribund to the very centre of the system: the Soviet Union. By spring 1989, the Soviet Union had not only experienced a lively media debate but had actually held its first multi-candidate elections (20 March 1989). For the first time since 1945 the wind of liberalization was blowing from East to West.

Meanwhile Honecker's regime in East Berlin tried to stifle the new Soviet influence by censoring Soviet newspapers. Soon both Poland and Hungary followed Gorbachev's example and broke with hard-line communists. Hungary then dismantled the Iron Curtain in July 1989, making way for emigration, enticing East Germans who were vacationing there to bolt for freedom. Aging and ill, Honecker refused to recognize the crisis of his regime.

Honecker's politburo comrades half-heartedly intrigued to replace him but waited until Gorbachev affirmed that the Kremlin would not back any clampdown on protests before acting on 18 October 1989.

By then huge peaceful protests were becoming a daily feature of East German life. The new leaders tried to rescue the situation even agreeing to let East Germans travel freely but within minutes of announcing the principle on 9 November 1989, scores of thousands of East Berliners converged on the crossing point to the west at Checkpoint Charlie. The authorities lost all control.

Now able to meet their West German cousins freely, the slogans of the demonstrations changed from "We Are the People" to "We Are One People." Free elections were set for 18 March 1990, but the attractions of economic and political union with the rich West would defeat any party, communist or not.

Unification was inevitable once the communists lost power. As one East German ideologist noted in August 1989: "Poland would remain Poland even if communism fell, but without communism East Germany had no reason to exist." Gorbachev's willingness to renounce the Soviet empire was the key trigger to the upheaval.

The collapse of the East German regime was a sign of crisis for the whole Soviet system. On the one hand, East Germany had been presented as the most modern and industrialized communist state in Europe and yet in reality it turned out to be hopelessly behind West Germany in terms of productivity and innovation, leaving aside personal freedom. Equally demoralizing for communist rulers was the Kremlin's willingness to abandon such a strategically vital ally, one where there were 600,000 Soviet troops. The fall of the East German regime crushed the idea that there was a viable socialist alternative to capitalism and marked a dramatic retreat by the Soviet superpower and a fundamental shift in international relations, which until 1989 had been dominated by the East-West divide running through Berlin itself.

7 October 1949
Soviet occupation zone declared German Democratic Republic

17 June 1953
Workers' uprising in East Berlin suppressed by Russians

13 August 1961
Building of Berlin Wall

1985

7 October 1989
40th anniversary of German Democratic Republic

9 October 1989
Huge crowd in Leipzig chants "We are the People"

18 October 1989
Resignation of Honecker, replaced by Egon Krenz

4 November 1989
Huge demonstration in East Berlin

9 November 1989
Opening of Berlin Wall

18 November 1989
Resignation of Politburo

1990

18 March 1990
Free elections produce pro-unification majority

1 July 1990
Currency union between the two Germanies

3 October 1990
Unification of East and West Germany as one state

ROMANIA

Romania's Christmas Revolution in 1989 was the most dramatic of the East European revolutions – a violent upheaval that ended in tyrannicide. The revolution's actual success raised questions about whether there had been a coup under cover of the people's protests. Unlike other East European countries, Romania had never undergone even limited de-Stalinization. Nevertheless Nicolae Ceausescu became leader of its Communist Party in 1965 and a grotesque personality cult developed. By 1989, Romanians suffered their media regurgitating the daily doings and speeches of Nicolae Ceausescu, quoting all of his titles, plus epithets like "Most Beloved Son of the Romanian People". The country's resources were poured into gigantic building projects to glorify Ceausescu's memory. Meanwhile Ceausescu reduced living standards drastically to pay off foreign debts incurred by earlier modernization schemes. Romania's impoverishment came to light after 1989, revealing the terrible plight of abandoned children in orphanages and the level of HIV infection. Romania set out on the post-communist road with one of the worst inheritances from the past.

Unlike the other Warsaw Pact leaders, Ceausescu had not been slavishly pro-Soviet but had pursued an independent foreign policy. While Gorbachev spoke of reform, Ceausescu imitated the political hard line and megalomania of East Asian communist leaders like Mao and North Korea's Kim II Sung. Even after the Berlin Wall fell and Ceausescu's southern comrade, Bulgaria's long-serving communist leader, Todor Zhivkov, was replaced on 9 November 1989, Ceausescu had himself re-elected unanimously as Romanian leader and ignored the threat to his position as the last old-style communist leader by leaving the country to go to Iran on a state visit.

As Ceausescu prepared to go to Tehran, his Securitate ordered the arrest and exile of a local Hungarian-speaking Calvinist priest, Laszlo Tökes, on 16 December for sermons offending the regime. The police seized Tökes but only after serious rioting had led to several deaths. Knowing from Western radio stations what had happened, a now-or-never spirit gripped many Romanians facing another grim hungry winter. Demonstrations spread. When Ceausescu returned from Iran he ordered a mass rally in his support outside Communist Party headquarters in Bucharest. To his astonishment, the crowd booed as he spoke. The television broadcast was cut, but viewers had seen their all-powerful leader humiliated.

At first the security forces obeyed Ceausescu's orders to shoot down protesters, but on the morning of 22 December the Romanian Army suddenly changed sides. Instead of patrolling the streets its tanks moved towards Party Headquarters with crowds swarming after them. Shocked, Ceausescu and his wife, Elena, his real second in command, fled by helicopter just as crowds burst into the building.

Elation at the flight of the Ceausescus was tamed by people's uncertainty about what had happened to them. Worse still, as night fell on 22 December gunfire began to echo around Bucharest and it seemed that Ceausescu loyalists were trying to recover power. On Christmas Day Romanian television showed the Ceausescus facing a hasty trial and then suffering summary execution. With their deaths, the apparent resistance of the Ceausescu loyalists died down.

However, more questions surfaced when it was revealed that Ceausescu's last defence minister, General Stanculescu, had been one of the judges at his trial. Many Romanians came to believe that their heroism in the streets provided a convenient cover for Ceausescu's disgruntled servants to topple him and his corrupt family.

The National Salvation Front (NSF) installed itself as Romania's new government under acting President Ion Iliescu, who charted a course for Western integration. In the run up to "free" elections set for 20 May, the NSF controlled the media and local government. Most Romanians were so grateful for the fall of Ceausescu that they would have backed Iliescu anyway, but a small number of students and leaders tried to block former Communist Party leaders, including Iliescu, from holding high office. They staged a sit-in in central Bucharest throughout the campaign and refused to leave after the elections. On 13 June the police failed to remove them, rioting followed, and President Iliescu called in a miners' militia that went on the rampage, dispersing the protesters but also tarnishing Romania's democratic image. Iliescu remained the central figure in Romanian politics for more than a decade, being re-elected for the third time in 2000. The survival of Ceausescu's one-time number two brought out the ambiguity of the Romanian revolution, at once the most violent in 1989 and yet the one that changed the least.

1985

1990

2-4 August 1977
Strike by miners in Jiu Valley – Ceausescu meets them

16 December 1989
Crowds gather outside home of Laszlo Tökes

18 December 1989
Ceausescu flies to Iran on state visit

21 December 1989
Ceausescu's speech disrupted by Bucharest crowd

22 December 1989
Nicolae and Elena Ceausescu flee but are captured

25 December 1989
Trial and execution of Nicolae & Elena Ceausescu

20 May 1990
National Salvation Front wins majority in elections – Ion Iliescu confirmed as president

13-14 June 1990
Ion Iliescu sets miners on student protestors in Bucharest

THE SOVIET UNION

It was only when Mikhail Gorbachev, the youngest member of the ruling Communist Party's Politburo, was elected general-secretary in March 1985, that the stagnation of the Soviet system became the subject of official concern: why wasn't the Soviet Union fulfilling its revolutionary promise? By the mid-1980s Soviet labour productivity was falling well behind the West and life expectancy was dwindling, in part due to alcoholism and pollution. The Chernobyl nuclear power plant catastrophe in April 1986 dramatically indicated the poor state of Soviet technology. Gorbachev's attempt to revitalize the Soviet system was too little too late. Although he talked about restructuring, he made no significant changes to the state-run economy, possibly hoping that loans from the West would fund effective reforms without changing the communist system into a market one. At the same time his liberalization of the media allowed decades of frustration and disillusionment with the system to surface after years of repression.

Already in 1988 Estonia became the first Soviet republic to declare itself sovereign. The next year Lithuania and Latvia followed suit. The collapse of the East European communist regimes with Gorbachev's consent encouraged other republics to seek self-government. When Russia, the largest republic, began to see itself as a victim of the Soviet system, the chances of Gorbachev's reforms succeeding took a nose dive.

Gorbachev had hoped free elections would let him remove corrupt and incompetent time-servers from the Soviet system but a significant number of serious critics of Gorbachev were elected in the March 1989 elections. The most important was Boris Yeltsin, Gorbachev's former protégé who had fallen out with him over the pace of reform in October 1987. Yeltsin was the most important example of the East European phenomenon of the communist official who turned against the Party in the late 1980s and advocated a completely new system based on Western market models.

Pressed by hardliners to clamp down, Gorbachev wavered. Early in 1991, he consented to violent action by pro-Soviet extremists in Lithuania and Latvia to try to reverse their pro-independence moves, but by the summer, he shifted to a conciliatory line.

Gorbachev soon found himself in a quandary. Yeltsin had seized the high ground of reform in Russia and had become the first directly elected president of that republic in June 1991, while Gorbachev's power stemmed from his indirect election as general-secretary of the Communist Party to the post of Soviet president in 1989. With Yeltsin denying his democratic legitimacy on one side, hard-line communist leaders criticized Gorbachev as soft.

In August 1991, the crisis came to a head. On 22 August a new constitution for the Soviet Union was due to be signed. Gorbachev agreed to allow the republics their independence. The hardliners, including Gorbachev's vice-president and premier, staged a half-hearted coup to stop it coming into force. Although they arrested Gorbachev at his holiday home, they failed to detain Boris Yeltsin, who made a dramatic public appearance on top of a tank outside his headquarters – the Russian White House in Moscow. The fact that soldiers allowed Yeltsin on to their tank showed how shallow was the support for the coup, and within three days it collapsed.

Yeltsin's speeches and energetic opposition made him the hero of the hour. When Gorbachev returned to Moscow, Yeltsin had seized the initiative. He was quick to offer the presidents of the other republics full independence. This left Gorbachev with a shadow position as head of a state whose members were rapidly declaring independence. His position as head of the Communist Party had effectively been abolished.

In December 1991, Yeltsin met with the presidents of Ukraine and Belarus to establish a Commonwealth of Independent States to replace the Soviet Union. With this, the Soviet Union died and Gorbachev resigned on 25 December 1991. It was an anticlimactic end to more than 70 years of one-party rule. However the aftermath was far from simple.

Although the individual republics became independent states, many of them faced separatist nationalities, like the Chechens, who demanded independence from Russia. Unlike some of the Central European post-communist countries, Russia and the majority of ex-Soviet republics failed to establish working market economies and genuinely democratic elections. The rhetoric of reform and democracy often hardly hid ambition and unscrupulous methods. Boris Yeltsin's resignation at New Year 2000 reflected the sense of bankruptcy associated with his erratic record, and his appointment of the former KGB officer, Vladimir Putin, as his successor seemed to mark a step back to the Soviet past.

1991

12 June 1991
Boris Yeltsin first democratically elected President of Russia

19-22 August 1991
Hardline coup against Gorbachev in USSR

8 December 1991
Presidents Yeltsin of Russia, Kravchuk of Ukraine, and Shushkevich of Belarus form Commonwealth of Independent States

25 December 1991
Mikhail Gorbachev resigns – end of Soviet Union

26 December 1991
Abolition of Soviet Union

1992

1 January 1992
End of price controls in Russia – start of "shock therapy"

1993

21 September–4 October 1993 *Yeltsin's forces besiege Moscow White House*

2000

Janaury 2000
Boris Yeltsin resigns and appoints Vladimir Putin as his successor

Serbia 2000

Slobodan Milosevic, the Serbian president after 1987, was the great survivor of the collapse of communism in Eastern Europe. As communist leaders across the region lost office in 1989, and the Soviet Union collapsed in 1991, Milosevic was able to transform himself from a communist *apparatchik* into a Serb national leader as Yugoslavia broke up into its component republics in 1991–2.

Richer republics in the north-west like Slovenia and Croatia had long resented subsidizing poorer ones, particularly federal funding of Serbian police repression in the mainly Albanian-inhabited province of Kosovo.

In early 1987, Milosevic had become a Serbian national hero by defending the minority Serbs in Kosovo against alleged persecution by the local Albanian majority. This stand catapulted him into the leadership of the Serbian Communist Party, soon renamed Socialist to give it a more reformed image. Milosevic revoked Kosovo's autonomy inside Serbia by taking over Kosovo's seat on the six-person rotating presidency of Federal Yugoslavia, and using federal troops to suppress protest after 1989.

Serb minorities lived in other Yugoslav republics and in 1991 Milosevic backed those in Croatia who resisted the victory of the pro-independence Croatian Democratic Union (HDZ) in the May 1990 elections. Clandestinely, he also helped emerging Bosnian Serb militias attack the Muslim-Croat majority who voted for independence in a referendum in February 1992.

UN SANCTIONS HELP STOP WAR

Although Milosevic avoided direct Serbian military intervention, Belgrade's role in supplying much of the finance and some of the weapons to the Bosnian Serbs led to UN sanctions, which led to hyperinflation and declining living standards.

Brutal "ethnic cleansing" by Serbian forces from the start of the war against Croatia in 1991 and throughout the Bosnian War became undeniable in July 1995 when the Muslim enclave of Srebrenica was overrun and Bosnian Serb television showed General Mladic personally organizing the separation of 7,000 Muslim men from their women and children. Most of the men have never been seen again and this atrocity finally stirred NATO countries to threaten military intervention to stop the war.

In summer 1995, Milosevic made peace with the US-led coalition, which wanted to

---

1987 Milosevic defends Serbs in Kosovo – becomes national hero

9 March 1991 Anti-communist demonstrations in Belgrade suppressed

1992–5 Bosnian War leads to UN sanctions on rump Yugoslavia

28 June 1989 Milosevic addresses 600th anniversary rally in Kosovo

1990

25 June 1991 Slovenia declares independence – break-up of Yugoslavia

21 November 1995 Dayton Agreement signed by Milosevic ends Bosnian War

stop the war in Bosnia, in order to get sanctions lifted which were hurting his power base in Serbia. He then turned his back on radical nationalist allies in Bosnia by signing the Dayton Peace Accords in November 1995. Milosevic offended both the Serbian nationalist movement and ordinary people who, despite the end of the war, continued to get poorer.

In autumn 1996, the previously splintered opposition parties united for the first time in the Zajedno ("Together") coalition to compete in local elections. They represented a wide range of anti-Milosevic opinion. At first the election commission refused to publish correct results. Huge demonstrations followed the electoral fraud for more than two months as crowds protested daily in Belgrade. At last in February 1997, Milosevic agreed to a law revising the results in cities like Belgrade, conceding the opposition's win.

Two key Zajedno leaders, Vuk Draskovic and Zoran Djindjic, soon quarrelled. It was rumoured that Milosevic had secretly bought them off because he needed to split such a powerful electoral force, which challenged his government's chances of winning future national elections. Certainly both had ambitions to run for the Serbian presidency in autumn 1997, and Draskovic felt cheated by Djindjic's refusal to back his candidacy despite the fact that Djindjic had received

the prize position of mayor of Belgrade after Milosevic acknowledged the election results.

Kosovo had simmered throughout the wars between Serbs, Croats, and Muslims in the early 1990s but only in late 1997 did a Kosovar Albanian liberation struggle get under way. Supporters of a self-styled Kosovo Liberation Army began attacking Serb police and so-called "collaborators". The Serb authorities responded with a harsh crackdown.

Alarmed by the prospect of another Balkan civil war, the NATO countries pressured Milosevic to refrain from reprisals for KLA attacks. Claims of a Serbian police massacre of Albanian civilians at Racak in January 1999 upped the tension. While the KLA was ready to agree to a NATO-led occupation of Kosovo to keep the peace, Milosevic rejected the proposals as the prelude to the occupation of Yugoslavia.

Confident that Milosevic would back down after a few air strikes, on 24 March 1999 NATO began a three-month-long bombing campaign. Milosevic's forces evicted more than 750,000 Albanians, creating a refugee crisis.

Milosevic pursued a highly personal policy. He had refused the pre-war US proposals, suspecting the US wanted to topple him by deploying NATO soldiers in Yugoslavia. However, in June 1999, after reassurance that NATO would not enter Serbia, he accepted a revised package of US demands, abandoned the Serbs of Kosovo, and left NATO in occupation of Kosovo under a UN mandate, but with Serbia under his control.

Ironically, Milosevic's withdrawal from Kosovo was a key factor in his downfall, not because it exposed the bankruptcy of his hard-line policies, but because many of the police and paramilitaries implementing them resented his decision to capitulate to the NATO demands once it was agreed that NATO-led KFOR troops would operate only

inside Kosovo. This removed the chance of NATO soldiers whisking Milosevic off to The Hague international tribunal for war crimes from "ethnic cleansing" in Kosovo.

Successive defeats alienated many of the Serb paramilitary hardliners from Milosevic. He was accused of selling out Serbs firstly in Croatia, then Bosnia, and now in Kosovo. The exodus of half the Albanian population earlier in 1999 was replaced by an almost complete flight of Serbs from the province once NATO arrived. Milosevic's Serbia now housed almost a million Serbs displaced from other parts of the former Yugoslavia.

Milosevic despised the quarrelling opposition parties and underrated the threat they posed to his regime. Deluded by his own propaganda that he was Serbia's only saviour, he moved to confirm his position as president of Yugoslavia in summer 2000 with a direct election. That gave his opponents at home and abroad the chance to topple him.

US polling agencies found that Vojislav Kostunica, the leader of the small Democratic Party of Serbia, was the least compromised politician in the country. Milosevic was unpopular and widely blamed for the flagging economy and corruption. Unlike other opposition leaders, like Draskovic and Djindjic, Kostunica had not been discredited by public squabbles and accusations of profiteering. Kostunica had a strongly nationalist record, condemning the

In protest over election fraud, unstoppable demonstrators set the Yugoslav parliament building in Belgrade on fire, 5 October 2000.

NATO bombing, when he stayed in Belgrade while Djindjic had taken refuge in Montenegro.

Kostunica's appeal for public trust gained ground and Milosevic's attacks on him as a NATO puppet lacked credibility. (Djindjic was kept off the campaign platform but was running the operation from behind the scenes). An opposition student movement "Otpor" ("Resistance") received generous subsidies from the US and a large supply of spray paint to daub the walls of Serbian towns with anti-Milosevic slogans.

On election day, 24 September 2000, it was clear that Kostunica would come first. The failure of the election commission to publish prompt results and its announcement three days later that Kostunica had fallen short of an absolute majority, so a second round would be needed, angered Serbs who feared another election fraud.

Djindjic's group had already contacted Serbian security forces, playing on their disillusionment with Milosevic and offering them a secure future. Industrial workers and miners went on strike to protest against the official plan to hold a second round of voting and falling living standards, defying attempts by the police to break their picket line. At the same time, an opposition mayor, Velimir Ilic, organized a convoy of men to come to Belgrade with a bulldozer to smash any barriers set up to block the protesters' march on 5 October.

By mid-afternoon it was clear that the police were not equipped to control the well-organized crowd and that the army was not willing to send in its tanks. The federal parliament was stormed and set ablaze and soon afterwards the headquarters of Serbian television was rammed by the bulldozer and its director beaten by an angry mob.

Milosevic followed events in a daze, and Kostunica was proclaimed president by the supreme court. On 6 October, Milosevic met the Russian foreign minister who mediated a handover of office to Kostunica.

MILOSEVIC SURRENDERS

Expectations of Western aid to repair the damage of sanctions and the previous year's massive bombing met with disappointment. The NATO states demanded Milosevic's transfer to The Hague Tribunal before paying out aid and felt less need to do so now that their bête noire had fallen.

The United States set the new regime in Belgrade a deadline for the arrest of Milosevic and his transfer to The Hague. Even then his successor, President Kostunica, was unwilling to hand him over, but Djindjic overruled him and sent Milosevic to The Hague on 28 June 2001.

Disentangling Serbia from the legacy of Milosevic's rule and the issues raised by the break-up of Yugoslavia was a formidable challenge for the politicians who came to power in October 2000, but who had been united only in opposition to Milosevic. So much violence and disruption had marked the years since 1991 that Milosevic's disappearance from politics was not a cure-all, even if some had thought it would be on 5 October 2000.

COUPS D'ÉTAT

Introduction

Although human history has been pockmarked by violent seizures of power and the murder or imprisonment of one deposed ruler by the next, the coup d'état is a modern development. From the earliest recorded human past, rival claimants to a dynastic throne have challenged each other's right of inheritance. The English Wars of the Roses (1461–85) in the 15th century, or for that matter, the Hundred Years' War between England and France (1340–1453), which preceded them, were essentially family quarrels about who should rule. Every trick of force and deceit was acceptable, but only under the sanction of the claim by one or other pretender to the throne that he was king by divine right.

BRUTE FORCE OVER DIVINE RIGHT

In contrast, the modern coup d'état relies completely on force, rather than an appeal to divine right, as the way to legitimacy. Revolutions always involve violence – as Mao noted, power grows out of the barrel of a gun – but there is a sharp difference between revolutionaries who come to power after a long armed struggle, like Mao or Castro, and those who use a single dramatic blow to put themselves in power. In a coup d'état force alone determines the outcome of the political struggle.

THE FIRST COUP D'ETAT

The first modern coup d'état was Napoleon Bonaparte's seizure of power in France on 9 November 1799 or 18 Brumaire (Foggy month) of Year VII, to use the revolutionary calendar then in force in France. The Republic had been convulsed by revolution, war, civil war, and hyperinflation since July 1789. Before he was 30, Napoleon had won a shining reputation as a republican general who had routed the apparently superior armies of states, like imperial Austria, and overrun much of Italy for France. Returning from his occupation of Egypt in 1799, Napoleon sensed the political instability and disillusionment with revolution in France. He also saw that discontent with the Republic did not necessarily mean nostalgia for the old order. What sufficiently large numbers of French people wanted was restored peace.

Almost by improvisation, Napoleon devised the format of the classic coup d'état. He realized that he needed to incapacitate the existing political elite without provoking resistance or chaos. As a first effort, Napoleon used reliable troops who owed him personal loyalty after sharing many campaigns with him, but his plan almost failed when the politicians, whom his men had surrounded, came close to lynching him before they were dispersed. Napoleon was, however, a master of

Boasting the strength of left-wing resistance, this 1930s Spanish Civil War poster illustrates the "Invincible Strength of the Proletariat Against Bullying Military Force".

targets. Having acquired the loyalty of troops and police, the coup-master had to isolate and arrest the existing government and cut its ability to arouse resistance. Similar tactics were used on 2 December 1851 when the newspaper editors of Paris found themselves rounded up for an uncomfortable winter's night in the cells with the politicians, detained by Napoleon's nephew, who was intent on establishing his dictatorship – the restored empire (1852–70). Without a central headquarters from which to organize and coordinate activities, resistance to such a coup was brief and scattered.

THE APPEAL OF MILITARY MESSIAHS

The Napoleonic model of the general turned (self-proclaimed) national saviour turned out to have wide appeal to military men. After decolonization, many new republics and newly independent states in 19th-century Latin America and then in Africa failed to establish popular and economically stable governments. This opened the door to many would-be Napoleons who could challenge these new unstable governments.

Post independence from colonial rule, Latin America saw a number of imitators of the Napoleonic precedent. Like his French model, the Mexican general Agustin de Iturbide, who did so much to win Mexican independence from Spain, proclaimed himself emperor in 1822. He was deposed in a coup the following year by the self-proclaimed "Napoleon of the West", Antonio Santa Anna. Mexican history entered an unhappy cycle of

improvisation and propaganda and he presented the coup as a decisive blow to end confusion and turmoil.

In an age before mass communications, Napoleon, like his nephew Louis-Napoleon 52 years later, had a relatively simple set of

coup and counter-coup, which set the turbulent model for much of Spanish speaking America.

The parade of short-lived military regimes led by grandiloquent leaders, who were better at matching Napoleon's capacity for plunder than military glory, is a dreary feature of the last 200 years in much of the developing world.

Napoleon's regime, however, was an example of one that came to power by force and with little popular consent, but which set about a grand project of creating a new order in France and then much of Europe. Dictatorial though Napoleon certainly was, his regime developed the legal codes and administrative system that underpinned French life for the next two centuries. For all his pomp and his adoption of the megalomaniac title of Emperor of the French (endorsed by a rigged referendum), and the terrible human cost of his wars, Napoleon, unlike so many other putschists, left a positive legacy to weigh, at least in part, against the negative effects of his rule.

Few others who have come to power by ruthless military means have matched Napoleon's wide-ranging achievements, though some have approached and exceeded the devastating cost inflicted on humans.

The Chilean general, Augusto Pinochet, staged a model modern coup d'état in 1973 against his socialist president, Salvador Allende. Pinochet was an anti-Marxist whose regime aimed to snuff out the radical left by terror but also to create a new viable capitalist market order in Chile, unlike the chaotic, corrupt, inflationary military regimes in neighbouring Argentina or Uruguay.

As a technician of the coup, Pinochet had few rivals. He targeted the key institutions of the modern state – the presidential palace, opposition party, and union headquarters and the radio and television – and seized them within a few hours.

Only the Polish communist general, Vojtech Jaruzelski, staged a similarly effective coup in modern times when he clamped down on the Solidarity opposition movement on 13 December 1981, in what Latin Americans would call an *auto golpe* – when a regime already in power uses force to keep itself there. Jaruzelski used a military coup to prevent the fall of the communist regime. Within hours of its start, the Polish security forces had effectively disrupted the opposition mass movement by arresting its leader, Lech Walesa, and hundreds of key organizers. Simultaneously all telephone communications were cut, leaving the population unable to organize a response.

The fall of communism in Poland eight years later, like Pinochet's eventual failure to get popular support, proved the wisdom of Talleyrand's comment to Napoleon after his coup – "You can do anything with bayonets, except sit on them." The people's loyalty could not be won by force alone – economic or other benefits were needed.

The fiasco of the attempt by communist hardliners in August 1991 to stop the democratization process in the Soviet Union reveals that it takes more than formal control of the levers of power to carry out a successful coup. By summer 1991, many Soviet soldiers and secret policemen no longer identified with the communist regime. The would-be putschists were chiefs without Indians to back the clampdown.

As with other aspects of revolution, it is frequently impossible to make an absolute separation between how a revolution achieves power at the moment of toppling the old regime and features of a coup d'état. Elements of a coup d'état can be found in even the most popular or ideological revolutions.

Take the Bolshevik Revolution in Russia in November 1917, for example. It is certainly true that there was an enormous amount of dynamism behind the appeal of a completely new communist society, especially to industrial workers in big cities like the capital St Petersburg, but Lenin and Trotsky went about the preparations for their seizure of power with all the methodical concern for detail of a classic military general staff.

The Italian fascist writer, Curzio Malaparte, took the Bolshevik storming of the Winter Palace in St Petersburg as the model for a coup d'état in his book *Technique of the Coup d'État*, which sets out the rules for an effective takeover of the heart of any government. Mussolini himself studied the way Trotsky's Red Guards had isolated Kerensky's provisional government inside the Winter Palace by occupying the telegraph agency and telephone operators' buildings. The Red Guards also took charge of key transport nodal points like bridges over St Petersburg's many canals, and the railway stations. In October 1922, Mussolini sent his Blackshirt militia to do much the same in Rome, in preparation for an uprising against the Italian state if it defied him.

The contrast between the coming to power of fascism in Italy and communism in Russia was the absence of any broad base of popular support for Mussolini's movement compared with Lenin's. Elections before October 1922 showed that Mussolini's party had only about seven per cent of the popular vote. Even though Lenin's Bolsheviks only gained just over one-quarter of the vote in the elections for the constituent assembly held in autumn 1917, in big cities like the capital there is little reason to doubt that they had a majority. It was in the cities, rather than the countryside, that political power lay.

WHY REGIMES BUILT ON FEAR FAIL

Mussolini's regime in Italy was not the first example of a political movement that came to power by force and intrigue with minimal popular support, and then used its control of the state machinery to promote an image of the regime as dynamic and popular. The reality became apparent when it faced adversity in World War II. As Mussolini's ally, Hitler, sneered, "What is this fascism which melts like snow before the spring sun?" Coups may create regimes by force, but unless they offer something more than fear, their lack of social roots and popular loyalty means they are doomed when confronted by greater force.

Italy 1922

Italian fascism was the first political movement in Europe to capitalize on the fear of communism after the Russian revolution in 1917, as well as on the disappointment felt by many war veterans at the results of World War I. Although after 1918 Italy was a maelstrom of social and economic problems and competing ideologies, the emergence and success of fascism would have been unthinkable without the role of one man – Benito Mussolini.

MUSSOLINI BREAKS WITH MARXISM

Mussolini's biography brought together in one person the contradictory strands of Italian society that made up the fascist movement after 1919. Born into a poor blacksmith's family and named by his radical father in honour of the Mexican executioner of an emperor, Benito Juarez, the young Mussolini became a radical schoolteacher, draft-dodger, and Marxist journalist. Mussolini's skill with words made him one of the 20th century's first master propagandists. He graduated from newsprint to the radio and then cinema, successfully using each form of media as a sophisticated instrument of persuasion and indoctrination.

Yet Mussolini was a deeply contradictory character. Having started his career by moving to the extreme left of Italian politics, Mussolini advocated a communist revolution against the parliamentary monarchy and denounced nationalism. But suddenly in 1914 he broke with his left-wing comrades and became the most vocal advocate of Italian entry into World War I.

A NEW KIND OF NATIONALISM

Mussolini's break with Marxism did not mean that he entirely abandoned his left-wing heritage. He claimed that his new nationalism and support for Italian entry into the World War I would create a crisis of the existing system. His thesis was that Italy would only be able to fight a great war by adopting socialist methods of mass organization. Militarization of society or entering the war would be the back door to social revolution.

Mussolini may well have believed that, but in order to fund his breakaway newspaper and embryonic political party he was willing to take money from big Italian arms manufacturers, like Fiat, and the British and French governments who were happy to

Poet and fascist, Gabriele d'Annunzio, watches a procession of Mussolini's fascists from the balcony of the prefect headquarters in Milan, 1922.

bribe anyone willing to fight Germany. Like many Italian politicians, Mussolini was corrupt and cynical, but unlike them he was not complacent. In fact he was prepared to use the most radical methods in order to obtain power.

THE NEW FASCIST PARTY

After war service, Mussolini recognized that many ex-front-line soldiers resented the Italian politicians who had led them into war for what turned out to be so little gain. Playing on his own war wounds (obtained in an accident), Mussolini presented himself as the veterans' spokesman. In March 1919, he established his own political movement. It combined radical criticisms of Italy's elite with violent anti-communism and nostalgia for ancient Roman greatness. Mussolini adopted the Roman symbol of authority, the axe wrapped in whipping rods, or the *fasci*, as the icon of his new party, Fascism.

While Mussolini was busy establishing his Fascist Party, many of his ex-comrades in the Italian Socialist Party were moving further to the left, inspired by the example of the Soviets. Inflation and economic disruption led workers in many factories in northern Italy to go on strike and occupy the buildings, wresting control from the owners.

31 October 1922
Blackshirts march through Rome in triumph – Mussolini takes office

3 January 1925
Mussolini proclaims himself dictator

2 October 1935 *Italy invades Ethiopia*

10 June 1940 *Mussolini declares war on Britain and France*

8 September 1943
Italy surrenders to Allies – Germany invades Italy

17 June 1924
Opposition MPs boycott parliament

11 February 1929
Lateran Pact with Pope creates Vatican state

1930

5 May 1936 *Italian army captures Addis Ababa. Mussolini proclaims new Roman Empire*

1940

25 July 1940 *Mussolini arrested by King Victor Emmanuel – Fascist regime collapses*

28 April 1945
Mussolini captured and executed by Italian partisans

FASCIST SQUADS CONTROL UNREST

Although the strikers were often ex-soldiers, Mussolini's movement attracted the kind of veterans who were happy to break these strikes by force. In 1920, about 50,000 blackshirted Fascist supporters were formed into squads who attacked strikers and left-wing politicians and newspapers. The industrialists, who had backed Mussolini's pro-intervention campaign after 1914, were happy to pay his squads to suppress trade unions. Landowners also helped organize rural fascist squads to prevent unrest among Italy's millions of peasants.

Mussolini dropped the radical parts of his programme in favour of an anti-communist crusade. Although Italy's post-1919 governments were deemed liberal, they were content to use the fascist squads in their attempt to tame the labour unrest. The Italian police rarely intervened in this process, as fascists often intimidated or humiliated their opponents.

FASCISTS LOSE ELECTION

For all the dynamic and brutal activism of his supporters, and the fact that the government in Rome seemed complacent about fascists breaking the law, Mussolini's party did badly at the elections. Despite the introduction of proportional representation, the fascists failed to win any seats in 1920 and only gained 35 (seven per cent of the vote) in May 1921, when Liberal Premier Giolitti gave them his tacit support.

Mussolini recognized that membership of parliament gave his supporters certain advantages, such as immunity from arrest for their violent actions, but he also saw that elections were not likely to bring him to power. For that, a sharpening of Italy's internal crisis was needed. To some extent, the radical left played into his hands in 1921 by splitting the Socialist Party and setting up a Communist Party openly allied to Lenin's regime in Moscow.

Such a polarization of Italian politics served Mussolini well. Playing on fear of communism, his blackshirts were let loose, while in Rome the game of parliamentary musical chairs, which proportional representation favoured by permitting a host of small groups to get elected to parliament, saw another weak coalition government installed in February 1922.

MUSSOLINI UNDERESTIMATED

Ironically, both liberals and those on the left underrated Mussolini's abilities for the same reasons. His florid speeches and balcony posings made him appear a buffoon to his rivals. They failed to note how effectively he had tamed the hard men who made up his fascist squads and was able to make himself their Duce, or undisputed leader. Mussolini was an able intriguer, an effective orator, and a canny paramilitary organizer.

Despite what appeared to be militant posturing, Mussolini spent much of the late summer of 1922 in behind-the-scenes strategic negotiations with the Italian establishment, playing on its fears of the left. By mid-October, he was confident that enough of the Italian elite would back him as prime minister if he pushed the issue, and so threatened an armed insurrection which, if defeated, would open the way to a left-wing revolution. Only when confident that the army would not oppose the action, Mussolini launched the 40,000-strong army of blackshirts for a march on Rome at the end of the month.

THE MARCH ON ROME

On the night of 27–8 October 1922, blackshirts began to occupy key public

A triumphant 1933 portrait of Benito Mussolini by Gerardo Dottori shows the fascist leader rising from the hills of Italy, surrounded by the force of his military squadron.

buildings like telegraph offices, to give them control over communications in the coming crisis. The Italian prime minister, Luigi Facta, asked the king, Victor Emmanuel III, to declare a state of emergency and deploy troops to forestall Mussolini's seizure of power. The king seemed to agree, but in behind-the-scenes manoevres, Mussolini persuaded key royal advisers that once in office as prime minister he would disband his squads and pursue "sound" conservative economic policies. Rather than risk confrontation, the king ignored his elected cabinet's request for martial law and sacked Facta, replacing him with Mussolini.

To celebrate his appointment and to give the impression that he had seized power rather than been granted it, Mussolini still brought his blackshirts to Rome to parade in triumph. This so-called "March on Rome" became a fascist propaganda legend. Mussolini himself came by overnight train from his base in Milan to take the salute.

Mussolini's appointment as premier gave him an uneasy and somewhat limited form of power because he still had to deal with the non-fascist majority in parliament. Over the next two years, Mussolini staged a slow-motion coup d'état, clearing away constitutional restraints on his power. It was only in 1924 that force became inevitable and singular control would become the basis of his regime.

A TOTALITARIAN REGIME

The uneasy relationship between the paramilitary fascists and parliament came to a crisis in 1924 when a socialist MP, Giacomo Matteotti, who enraged Mussolini's men with his biting critique of their corruption and posturing, was kidnapped and murdered. Most of the opposition boycotted parliament, demanding Mussolini's resignation. After months of confusion, Mussolini decided to abandon any pretence of the rule of law, act openly like a dictator, and abolish the opposition parties in January 1925.

Now Mussolini proclaimed that his regime was "totalitarian". It would brook no opposition and every Italian was to be subordinate to the state. For all his grand claims about transforming Italy, while in power Mussolini's regime became increasingly conservative. It signed the Lateran Accords with the Pope, ending decades of discord between Italy and the Catholic Church. Mussolini himself got married in the Catholic Church and would celebrate 15 years of marriage. He even preached motherhood as a fascist virtue – "Every woman is by her natural destiny a mother" – but largely because he wanted to breed more young men for his planned future wars of conquest.

Mussolini wanted to mobilize Italy's resources to create a grand military power that would recover the long-lost status of the Roman Empire in the Mediterranean region. However, Mussolini mistook his rhetoric about Italian power for reality.

ITALY DECLARES WAR ON ALLIES

In 1935 he invaded Ethiopia, but only succeeded in defeating the poorly equipped

A group of soldiers from the Abyssinian Army (in Ethiopia) carry reinforced shields and rifles during the unwinnable war with Italy, March 1936.

Ethiopians by using terror tactics like poison gas. Instead of learning the lessons of Italy's poor preparation, Mussolini used up valuable Italian resources and sent 70,000 troops to fight in Spain in 1936.

Mussolini's megalomaniac unreality got worse as his German ally, Hitler, achieved lightening victories over Poland, the Low Countries, and then France, leading Mussolini to jump to the conclusion that the Allies were already defeated. So he declared war on France and Great Britain to grab his share of the spoils on 10 June 1940. Britain, however, continued the struggle and soon the hollowness of Italian military power was revealed in North Africa and by a disastrous invasion of Greece. German troops rescued the Italians at first but, as Hitler invaded the Soviet Union and then declared war on the United States in 1941, the balance of power shifted against the Axis states and Italian armies took terrible casualties.

At home, Mussolini's popularity plummeted and many fascists, generals, and the king began to look for ways to rescue themselves from the inevitable catastrophe. Mussolini's dictatorship had left the Italian monarchy in place as a puppet but once the Allies invaded Sicily, King Victor Emmanuel quickly ordered the Italian Army to arrest Mussolini after even his own fellow fascist leaders turned against him on 25 July 1943.

MUSSOLINI AND FASCISM DIE

A daring operation by German paratroops rescued Mussolini from prison, but he was a broken man. Now a puppet of the Nazis, he ran a shadow fascist regime called the Italian Social Republic in northern Italy. In reality the area he covered was the shrinking zone of Nazi occupation, which was slowly diminishing as the Allies advanced from the south. While Mussolini fantasized about achieving his early radical goals, his remaining loyalist blackshirts fought alongside the Germans in a savage civil war against the growing numbers of partisans who emerged from the communist underground and other left-wing forces. It was a much more brutal rerun of the quasi civil war between 1919 and 1922, and this time the left was winning along with its Anglo-American allies.

German defeat spelled the end for Mussolini, who was betrayed into partisan hands at the end of April 1945 and shot. Other leading fascist diehards were executed along with him and their bodies were displayed in Milan. Fascism as an organized political movement seemed dead, too.

Today in Italy, a so-called "post-fascist" party, the National Alliance, hovers around 15 per cent of the vote, and Mussolini's granddaughter Alexandra is one of its MPs. However, to gain what respectability it has, the National Alliance has had to ditch the most objectionable features of Mussolini's bullying, brutal tactics, and ambitions. It even supports full Italian integration into the EU rather than great power status for Italy.

Spain 1936–9

Like Russia before 1917, Spain in the early 1930s was a country in the throes of a transition to modernity but in which the balance between rural and industrial development was uneven. As the first major civil conflict in Europe since the Russian Civil War and the first major political upheaval since Hitler's Nazis had come to power in Germany in 1933, events in Spain took on a symbolic importance for the outside world as a battle between fascism and communism, a prelude to the coming World War II.

The Spanish Civil War broke out in July 1936, embodying that decade's three-way international struggle between fascism, communism, and democracy, but also the culmination of decades of internal disagreements about what sort of country Spain should be. Spain was a society with bitter social divides between the rich and poor, town and country. The very idea of a united nation was also hotly contested by minorities like the Basques and Catalans, who had their own language and distinct cultural identities. The traditional domination of the Catholic Church over religious and cultural life was questioned by liberal and left-wing anticlericals who blamed the church for Spain's intolerant past. Would-be crusaders defending the church regarded the abolition of the Inquisition in the 19th century as the beginning of the end of the old Spain that they wanted to restore.

AN UNSTABLE MONARCHY

Although Spain had avoided participation in World War I, it had been affected by the ideological and economic impact of the conflict. The monarchy had faced repeated challenges since the late 19th century, but political reform had been superficial. Spain had seen a lot of political instability since the mid-nineteenth century as rival claimants to the throne struggled for power and the new working class in cities like Barcelona combined with discontented peasants to see powerful revolutionary and anarchist movements emerge, albeit to be repressed by the army and police. The parliamentary system of the Spanish monarchy before 1923 barely masked these tensions. The formal liberal system failed to satisfy the growing radical left-wing and anarchist groups, and the ethnic minorities, and the reactionary right blamed it for destabilizing the country. King Alfonso XIII survived five assassination attempts – a telling index of Spain's instability.

13 September 1923 *Primo de Rivera made dictator by King Alfonso XIII*

14 April 1931 *King Alfonso XIII leaves Spain – Republic proclaimed*

January 1930 *Primo de Rivera resigns and dies shortly afterwards*

October 1934 *Franco brutally suppresses miners' strike in Asturias*

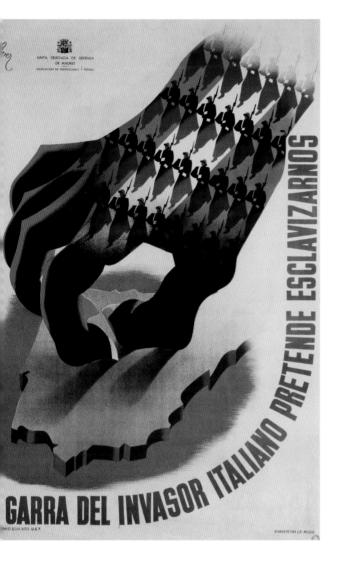

JUNTA DELEGADA DE DEFENSA
DE MADRID
DELEGACIÓN DE PROPAGANDA Y PRENSA

GARRA DEL INVASOR ITALIANO PRETENDE ESCLAVIZARNOS

"The Italian Invaders Want to Enslave Us." This propaganda poster during the Spanish Civil War depicts the fist of fascism with the red, white, and green of the Italian flag.

declared war to separate Cuba and the Philippines from Spain, the generation of Spaniards who came to adulthood before the civil war was deeply affected by Spain's decline as a formidable world power, including the ambitious young Francisco Franco, whose plans for a naval career were abruptly changed by the American annihilation of the Spanish fleet. Instead of the naval academy, Franco entered a military cadet school.

A DEMOCRATIC START

Although the young Franco distinguished himself in the fighting, Spain's defeat in a 1923 campaign to maintain control over Morocco, Spain's last colony, humiliated the liberal regime and enabled the king to appoint a dictator, Primo de Rivera. Rivera's goal was political order combined with government-sponsored economic progress, intended to mop up unemployment and undermine left-wing support. Primo de Rivera's regime was in many ways a pale version of Mussolini's fascism, but when ill health caused him to retire in 1930, democracy was restored.

Having lost most of her residual colonial empire in 1898, when the United States began its first great imperial expansion and

The first step to democracy was the holding of municipal elections on 12 April 1931. Early election results showed a surge of support for the left. By Tuesday, 14 April, crowds in big cities like Barcelona and Seville were proclaiming a republic. The army and

February 1936 Popular Front *ies win the general election*

8 May 1936 Azana elected *President of the Republic*

18 July 1936 *Beginning of military revolt – Franco flies to Spain*

28 March 1939 *Madrid falls to Franco's forces – end of civil war*

26 April 1936 *Nationalist planes bomb Basque town of Guernica*

13 July 1936 Murder of *Calvo Sotelo gives coup plotters an excuse*

1 October 1936 Franco *proclaimed "Generalissimo"*

1 April 1939 *United States recognizes Franco's government*

1940

even General Sanjurjo, the commander of the Civil Guards, traditionally the bastion of the regime, told Alfonso XIII that they would not intervene to suppress protests.

Alfonso XIII lost his nerve and fled into exile. But the fall of the monarchy soon exposed the reality that the new republic was not established on a consensus. Only a narrow, if vocal, majority supported the republic, particularly in the big cities, while large parts of Spain, especially rural areas, stood solidly against it.

The deepening world economic depression was also bad for the republic. Unemployment rose and businessmen and landlords experienced intense financial pressure. Landless peasants, who could no longer find work, agitated for land reform and occupied land. Public order came under strain as strikes, lockouts, and occupations became increasingly commonplace. In many small towns, previously unpoliticized people came into contact with urban agitators anxious to spread modern ideas of progress, including ideas promoting the rights of women, and those who had dominated rural society felt deeply threatened.

1934 ELECTIONS FAVOUR THE RIGHT

In 1934, the right won the general elections and began to restore order using heavy-handed methods. This provoked an uprising in northern Asturias in October 1934, where the youngest general in the Spanish Army,

English volunteers from the Independent Labour Political Party make their way from London to the International Brigades in Barcelona, 10 January 1937.

Francisco Franco, was let loose to command troops with whom he had earned his reputation as a colonial warrior in Morocco. Dismissing the opposition as "Moors" Franco achieved his mission but earned the hatred of the regional working class as a brutal militarist.

Despite the right's clampdown on trade unions and leftist activity in general, it respected the norms of parliamentary democracy and participated in fresh elections in February 1936. To the surprise of many, the vote swung to the left-wing Popular Front, which effectively united a broad coalition while right-wing parties frittered away their almost equal number of votes among competing groups.

Prime Minister Manuel Azana was remarkably complacent about the growing polarization of politics. Admittedly, since his Popular Front government contained no overtly Marxist ministers, it was true to say that it could hardly be classified as a pro-Soviet regime as the right accused it, but rational attitudes were fast disappearing.

Perhaps because the republic had survived a coup plot by the Civil Guards' commander General Sanjurjo in 1932, and the elections in February 1936 had been allowed to reverse the right's dominance, Azana thought that the rumours of a coup were exaggerated. In any case the police and the special Republican paramilitary Assault Guards were loyal. An additional factor leading him to feel over-confident was the fact that only four of the army's more than 20 generals were reported to be involved in plots and the most dangerous, Francisco Franco, was isolated on the Canary Islands out in the Atlantic.

On 16 July 1936 the radical right-wing leader Calvo Sotelo was murdered by Assault Guards who blamed him for the death of one of their comrades. Calvo Sotelo's murder was fortuitous for the pro-fascist military plotters. It gave them a high-profile victim to revenge and removed a potential political rival to any future military dictator. The army plotters were already prepared for action and the code words ordering a seizure of power were sent out. Radicals in Barcelona then did a similar favour for the generals in charge of the coup attempt by shooting José Antonio Primo de Rivera, the son of the late dictator and leader of the fascistic Falange, after a show trial in which the jury were asked if they "hated" the defendant.

The coup was dangerously fumbled at the start. Its intended commander, the exiled General Sanjurjo, was killed in a plane crash as he set out from Portugal to take charge of the insurgency. Key cities like the capital, Madrid, and Barcelona remained in government hands and joint Assault Guard/workers militia forces quickly massacred right-wing rebels. In fact the government counter-attack threatened to snuff out rebel centres like the Military Academy in Toledo before Franco's troops could reach them.

However, with the decisive aid of Italian and German planes, Franco was able to fly with Moroccan Legionnaires to Spain over the pro-Republican navy that blockaded any sea crossing. The arrival of these colonial veterans saved the putsch from collapse. It also radicalized the way that the civil war was fought. As Franco's Moroccan Legionnaires advanced on Madrid in August 1936, they routinely executed anyone found with evidence of rifle recoil bruises on their shoulders, and thousands who hadn't. The troops treated unenthusiastic Spaniards as they had Moroccan tribes people: the women were raped and the men were tortured and murdered. If such savagery was intended to terrorize Republicans into surrender it proved, ultimately, counter-productive. Thousands of city dwellers, especially in Madrid, hurried to form militias to resist the fascist rebels.

On the Republican side, the coup provoked an orgy of reprisals against groups identified with the right-wing rebels. The Catholic Church was particularly hard hit as its hierarchy in Republican territory was blamed for promoting the rebellion. Almost 7,000 priests, monks, and nuns were killed in the first few weeks of the civil war. Each side now had its martyrs to revenge. The claim by Franco's Nationalists, that in addition to four uniformed columns marching on Madrid they had a fifth column waiting inside the capital to rise up, convinced many Republicans of the necessity of a revolutionary purge.

ITALIANS AID NATIONALISTS

Italian aid proved vital in sustaining the Nationalists after their initial setbacks. Mussolini poured 70,000 "volunteers",

weapons, and ammunition into the rebel-held parts of Spain. Under the guise of "pirates", Italian submarines attacked ships travelling to Republican-held ports. Hitler sent only 15,000 troops, many of them airmen, but their expertise in the new arts of aerial warfare aided Franco's armies enormously. They were responsible for the first large-scale bomb damage in military history on towns like Guernica, the Basque capital, immortalized in Picasso's monumental anti-fascist painting.

While the fascist states openly backed the Spanish rebels, the two great democracies, Great Britain and France, soon adopted a policy of non-intervention, which hindered aid to the Republic without preventing Axis assistance to Franco. Despite official discouragement, many thousands of Western anti-fascists as well as communist exiles from Germany and Italy travelled to Spain to fight for the Republic in its International Brigades. The presence of poets and writers helped to create a moving record of the Republic's slow-motion defeat.

The Soviet Union also sent about 5,000 military advisers and some munitions, although Stalin's help proved to be a mixed blessing, being enough to taint the Republicans with the charge that they were communists, while not being enough to turn the tide of the war. The aid that he provided amounted to much less than that of Hitler and Mussolini's contributions to Franco. Also, his entrance into the fray seemed to justify the view of some that Spain was a cockpit for a struggle between competing totalitarian ideologies – namely, communism and fascism. Worse still, the Soviet advisers organized their own mini-civil war against the Republican camp by trying to purge real and imagined supporters of Stalin's exiled rival, Leon Trotsky. Much Republican effort was wasted on this internal power struggle while Franco consolidated his hold on power in the Nationalist zone.

REPUBLICAN RESISTANCE COLLAPSES

Whereas Franco effectively united the various reactionary and fascist forces into a single movement, the Republic was beset by intrigues between politicians, vicious struggles between communists and those they decried as Trotskyists or anarchists, and regional loyalties that saw Asturian, Basque, or Catalan units sacrifice the Republic's overall strategic interests to their local concerns. Franco eventually succeeded in splitting the Republican territory first in two, and then into three increasingly isolated enclaves.

After the initial failure of the coup, the war turned into a war of attrition. Franco's control of key food-producing areas, plus the ability of the Nationalists to trade while the Republican side was largely blockaded, meant that the war ground down the Republic more than the Nationalists. Shortages grew steadily worse in the big Republican cities.

By the end of 1938, the balance of power had shifted in favour of Franco's forces. Internal squabbles disorientated the Republicans more and more and in the early

spring of 1939, organized resistance collapsed and the Nationalists captured Barcelona and Madrid.

The civil war may have been over but Franco's forces went on an orgy of retribution to cleanse Spain of any trace of Republicanism and communism. Even Hitler's Gestapo chief, Heinrich Himmler, was taken aback by the scale of Franco's reprisals, which were still continuing in 1940. The war cost as many as 650,000 lives but well over 100,000 more were killed afterwards in what became known as the White Terror – Franco's period of widespread intimidation and retaliation.

World War II soon followed on the heels of its Spanish rehearsal. Although some guerrillas tried to carry on the struggle against Franco in the hope that his regime would be toppled with the defeat of Hitler and Mussolini, in fact after 1945 both the British and American democracies preferred to deal with Franco rather than risk a communist takeover in Spain as the Cold War with the Soviet Union began.

Franco's efforts to perpetuate his dictatorship after his death were clearly doomed to failure. In fact, after Basque terrorists murdered his prime minister, Admiral Carrero Blanco, in 1973, Franco admitted to his nominated successor, Juan Carlos, that "You will not rule as I have." The future king probably never had any intention of trying to imitate Franco. Instead he presided over a peaceful and skilful transition to full democracy in June 1977 – hardly 18 months after Franco's death.

Chile 1973

In the early 1970s, Chile was the only country in the Western hemisphere to came close to achieving a socialist transformation of society. It was also the scene of one of the most decisive and brutal military coups in Latin America in that coup-ridden epoch. However, unlike other Latin American countries that suffered a military dictatorship in this period (especially neighbouring Argentina), Chile's post-coup regime was more than just a generals' club running the country for their own benefit. After the suppression of Salvador Allende's experiment in socialism, General Augusto Pinochet subjected Chile to an equally radical experiment in the market economy. To their supporters and detractors inside and outside Chile, both Allende and Pinochet became personifications of ideological choices that brooked no compromise.

A PRESSURED WELFARE STATE

Unlike other Latin American countries, Chile had a long history of almost uninterrupted constitutional government in the 20th century. Chileans tended to look down on their neighbours with their frequent coups and revolutions. Although the Chilean Army had the reputation of being the Prussians of the continent – and its troops wore pre-World War I-style German uniforms on parade – it had proved reluctant to intervene in politics even in the long period of relative decline from the 1930s onwards.

By 1970, the chances of a radical challenge to the existing socio-economic system from the left had grown dramatically. Copper, the mainstay of Chile's export industry, was falling in price and, in any case, much of its profits were foreign, mainly in American hands. A growing population put pressure on employment and social services. Chile had developed quite an extensive welfare state and was now having difficulty funding it.

ALLENDE FOUNDS SOCIALIST PARTY

The champion of the left was Salvador Allende, a veteran socialist politician who did not hide his Marxist views. Born into a wealthy family in the port city of Valparaiso, Salvador Allende trained to be a doctor at Santiago University, where he first came into contact with Marxist ideas that came to shape his concerns about poverty. Allende had been among the Socialist Party's founders in 1933 and was first elected a

26 July 1908 Salvador Allende born in Valparaiso

1964 Allende runs for presidency and fails to win vote

4 September 1970 Allende elected president with 36.3 per cent of vote

3 November 1970 Allende inaugurated as president of Chile

25 November 1915 Augusto Pinochet born in Valparaiso

1967 Christian democrats pass Allende's land reform law

1970

24 October 1970 Chilean congress confirms Allende's election

March 1973 Allende's support win 44 per cent i congressional ele

deputy in 1937. He was appointed minister of health, a position he held briefly, before winning a seat in the senate, which he held from 1945 until 1970. Allende had already run unsuccessfully for president two times.

However, in 1964, he was only defeated because the right withdrew its candidate in favour of the Christian democrat, Eduardo Frei, whose programme was quite left-wing and appealed to many because of promises of land reform and workers' rights.

ALLENDE WINS PRESIDENCY

The United States had made Frei's government the model of what it called the Western hemisphere's "Alliance for Progress" and Washington granted Chile more aid per capita than any other state between 1964 and 1970. The Americans were bitterly disappointed when Salvador

An anti-Pinochet protester's shadow falls on a banner adorned with the pictures of Allende supporters who were "disappeared" in Chile.

6 May 1973 *Supreme Court finds against Allende's government*

22 August 1973 *Congress condemns illegal acts by popular unity*

11 September 1973 *Allende dies in military coup*

16 October 1998 *Senator Pinochet arrested in London*

3 March 2000 *Pinochet returned to Chile and tried for murder and kidnapping*

29 June 1973 *Premature tank coup in Santiago, the "tancazo"*

23 August 1973 *Allende appoints Pinochet head of army*

1980

6 December 1989 *Democracy restored in Chile – Patricio Aylwin elected president*

24 March 1999 *British House of Lords ruled that Pinochet had no "sovereign immunity"*

Allende, as the broad Left Popular Unity candidate, came first in the 1970 presidential election, albeit with only 36.3 per cent of the vote. The centre-right split its vote between Jorge Alessandri, with 34.9 per cent, and the Christian Democrat, Radimiro Tomic, who polled 27.8 per cent. The Christian democrats in Congress agreed to endorse Allende's win if he provided support for 10

An armed guard patrols a makeshift concentration camp where prisoners have been detained for questioning about their support of Allende at the National Stadium, Santiago.

constitutional amendments to secure freedom of speech and property rights under a Marxist president.

ALLENDE IMPLEMENTS CHANGE

Before Allende was inaugurated on 3 November 1970, the political situation began to destabilize. In October 1970, unknown assassins murdered the army's commander, General René Schneider. Extremists on both left and right were accused, the latter of removing a moderate general in the hope of provoking a coup by right-wing officers.

Allende actually implemented a land reform law passed by the Christian democrats in 1967, although it was only haltingly implemented before 1970. It allowed the state to redistribute farms of more than 80 hectares to landless peasants. Still it was a long way from Allende's Marxist dreams and those of popular unity militants.

Allende approved rapid wage rises that fuelled inflation and undercut the viability of key sectors of the economy. They also had a political impact. For instance, in parts of the non-state media, the wages bill and other costs rose at twice the rate of advertising revenue and several radio stations and newspapers were sold to popular-unity backers by owners who faced bankruptcy.

SOCIALIST WIN THREATENS US

The CIA had done very little to prevent Allende's victory, partly because its director, Richard Helms, regarded the Christian democrat candidate, Tomic, as a no-hoper: "You can't beat somebody with nobody," Helms wearily commented on Frei's doomed would-be successor. President Nixon, however, was furious at Allende's victory and already in October 1970, before Allende's inauguration, the US President told aides he was going to "smash that bastard Allende". His national security adviser, Henry Kissinger, told his staff as early as 27 June 1970, "I don't see why we need to stand by and watch a country go communist due to the irresponsibility of its own people."

Nixon and Kissinger saw Allende as least as bad for US interests as Cuba's Castro, and in some ways more dangerous because he was the first avowed Marxist to win an election fairly and squarely and therefore enjoyed much greater legitimacy than pure revolutionaries like Castro. The fact that Allende's daughter was married to a Cuban diplomat was viewed as sinister in Washington. Foreign businessmen from Venezuela, Mexico, Peru, and Brazil and the CIA channelled money to self-employed Chileans, like truck drivers who went on strike over inflation and government regulation, to keep them from work.

US BACKS PINOCHET COUP

Already in May 1973, CIA officers had urged one general, Augusto Pinochet, to act against Allende, but he had replied cautiously that the army should only intervene, "when up to its knees". He seemed to be implying that more disillusionment with the Popular Unity radicals was needed for a coup to succeed.

At the end of June 1973, some tank officers staged their own rather farcical coup. Army commander, General Prats, and Pinochet calmed the situation and returned troops to barracks. The failure of this "tancazo" had a dangerous side effect. More than 500 factories were occupied by workers and were controlled by Popular Unity radicals afterwards. Allende made only vague statements about returning them to their owners. A new wave of nationalization without congress approval seemed imminent.

ALLENDE TOPPLED

On 9 August, army commander, General Prats, entered Allende's cabinet as minister of defence but the generals voted that they had no confidence in him. On 23 August, Allende promoted Augusto Pinochet to commander-in-chief of the army, naively thinking him an apolitical general. The day before the congress voted a resolution condemning Allende's government for acting illegally and outside the constitution. Now Pinochet became the centre of the web of military conspiracy to topple Allende. Endorsed by Washington, the military commanders planned to surround Santiago with tanks while trusted troops seized the presidential palace, the Moneda in the city centre. Early on 11 September 1973, the armed forces began their attack, anticipating any Popular Unity counter-measures based on their response to the "tancazo" in June.

When his aides from the three armed

services tried to persuade Allende to surrender, since he was in a hopeless situation with the army and air force bombarding the presidential palace, he refused to do so and only offered to talk to the junta if they came to him. Equipped with a rifle and steel helmet like other militiamen in the Moneda, Allende assured the officers he would use his last bullet to shoot himself rather than surrender. He had failed to carry out peacefully and democratically what Castro had achieved in Cuba.

MILITARY JUNTA HOARDS POWER

Until about 10.30am, Santiago radio still broadcast Allende's last defiant statement. Although he urged resistance he did not demand suicidal actions by others. "I have faith in Chile... Other men will overcome this dark and bitter moment." He was anxious to avoid civilian casualties.

After Allende's death, Soviet leaders criticized his failure to infiltrate the armed forces with his own supporters to forestall any coup, but that was easier said than done. Ironically, loyal officers, like Prats, had refused to support a coup but also made sure that the professional officer corps was not politicized, at least not by the left.

The popular unity bloc was stunned by the savagery and speed of the military coup. Many other Chileans welcomed it because at first the military talked about restoring the normal constitutional order. This pacified the broad strand of parties and people who had criticized Allende sharply but wanted Chile

to remain democratic. However, it became clear within days that the junta had no intention of handing power back to congress. Soon enough other members of the junta were pushed aside so that power could be concentrated in General Pinochet's hands.

17 YEARS OF REPRISALS

In the immediate aftermath of the coup, the army set up a makeshift concentration camp in Santiago's football stadium where thousands of suspected Allende supporters were subjected to brutal questioning. The armed forces arrested about 130,000 people in the first few years after their coup. About 3,000 opponents of the new regime were executed or "disappeared" over the next 17 years, with the worst oppression in the early years after 1973. The Villa Garibaldi headquarters of the secret police became a dreaded destination for anyone arrested in Chile. The so-called "Caravan of Death" saw hundreds disappeared in the desert wastes of Chile while Operation Condor involved cooperation between Chile and other regional military dictatorships in "disappearing" mutual critics, including left-wing Americans and West Europeans who came to Chile to support Allende.

AN ECONOMIC COUNTER-REVOLUTION

Unlike military dictators across Latin America, Pinochet's regime did not just rest on bayonets and denouncing Marxism without offering any alternative strategy. He

General Pinochet in Cajon del Maipo, Chile, 7 September 1998, shortly before his visit to Britain, where he was arrested for genocide and torture under international law.

decided to start an economic counter-revolution of his own; Pinochet backed the proposals of a team of local economists, the so-called Chicago Boys, to adopt the radical free-market proposals of the US economist, Milton Friedman. Pinochet took up monetarism before Ronald Reagan or Margaret Thatcher had made it fashionable in the West. Savagely cutting government spending (except on the military), Pinochet both dismantled the welfare state and produced a boom of sorts for the top 40 per cent of the population.

PINOCHET VOTED OUT

However, economic growth was not enough to blot out memories of the coup or provide enough jobs for the growing population.

In March 1981, Pinochet assumed the presidency for a second eight-year term, but specified in his constitution that he could stand again if a referendum endorsed the idea. By the time the referendum came along, Chileans were not so easily swayed in their voting. The very success of his economic changes undermined Pinochet's power. The new Chilean middle class saw continued military rule as an obstacle to the country's full integration into the normal world. Even American policy now backed democratic governments and President Reagan's administration saw little chance of a radical left-wing regime replacing Pinochet.

Pinochet accepted defeat in Chile partly because his constitution granted him immunity as a senator-for-life from any criminal charges relating to his dictatorship. However in October 1998, on a visit to London for back surgery, Pinochet found that his immunity ended outside Chile. He was arrested for genocide and torture under international law. After his 18-month house arrest, Britain allowed him to return to Chile on health grounds. At home he was attacked in part because he had lost his terrifying aura while under arrest in Britain.

Portugal 1974

The Portuguese revolution in 1974 started as a revolt against the long-running wars to retain Portugal's African colonies, waged by the country's 50-year-old dictatorship. The US feared that rebellious junior officers would lead Portugal in a Communist direction, but the people of Portugal were anxious to break out from decades of self-imposed isolation at the hands of the right-wing dictatorship since 1926 and rejected a shift towards the Soviet Union. Instead Portugal became the first European country to make the transition from dictatorship to democracy as part of its accession to the European Community.

For much of the 20th century, one man, Antonio Salazar, ruled Portugal. In 1926, when he was appointed finance minister, Salazar effectively became head of the dictatorial regime, exerting vast influence over the rest of the government, which he formally headed from 1932 until 1968.

Salazar ran a low-key fascist regime in so far as his so-called New State allowed no political parties, promoted corporatism in the economy, and repressed political or trade-union dissent brutally. His regime had none of the populism of fascist Italy or Nazi Germany and did without the mass rallies that even Franco indulged in Spain. It was a quiet dictatorship, though it could be cruel to opponents, and suffocated free expression.

Salazar's Portugal sided with the Allies in World War II without actually fighting Nazi Germany, so the USA, and Britain treated Portugal favourably after 1945. As a bulwark against the spread of communism, not only at home but in Portugal's extensive African empire and as far away as East Timor, Salazar's regime was a valuable if junior Western ally in the Cold War. The Portuguese Azores provided the Americans with a valuable base in the middle of the Atlantic.

As age wore him down, Salazar handed over power in 1968 and died in 1970, by which time his regime was visibly decaying. His successor, Dr Marcello Caetano, lacked charisma and was unable to satisfy growing discontent with the system.

AFRICAN COLONIES REBEL

By 1970 Britain and France had granted independence to all but a handful of their colonial territories while Portugal continued to rule territories many times her own size. The only part of the Portuguese empire lost under the dictatorship was the port-city

---

5 July 1932
*Antonio Salazar appointed prime
minister with dictatorial powers*

September 1968
*Salazar transfers his powers
to Dr Marcello Caetano*

1945

April 1945
*Portugal enters war against Nazi
Germany and is admitted as founder
member of United Nations*

1960

enclave of Goa, which India seized in 1961. Salazar's Portugal could not fight India, but was determined to hold onto its vast African empire. Starting in February 1961, the Angolan People's Movement for the Liberation of Angola (MPLA) initiated a liberation struggle inspired by the end of Belgian rule in neighbouring Congo, setting off a chain of rebellions around the country. By September 1964, Frelimo, the Marxist Mozambiquean liberation movement, began a guerrilla war against Portuguese rule.

The pressures in Africa grew rapidly in the late 1960s. After 1967 Portuguese conscripts

In a 1961 broadcast, President Salazar speaks about Goa, a Portuguese colony on the west coast of India, which India took over without a fight.

faced four years in uniform including two years in one of the African colonies. At any one time up to 150,000 of Portugal's army of 180,000 were fighting the resistance movements in Angola, Mozambique, or Guinea. Many young men fled Portugal to live elsewhere in Western Europe rather than fight in Africa. The scale of draft dodging belied the regime's claim to be fighting a war in the national interest, defending integral parts of Portugal. Enrolment at the

---

15 May 1974
Spinola appointed president

25 June 1975
Portugal grants
Mozambique independence

25 November 1975
Communist takeover thwarted
by army and Socialists

12 August 1982
Last vestiges of military
political power removed
from constitution

24 April 1974
sident Caetano
hrown by army

1975

30 September 1974
Spinola replaced by Costa
Gomes as president

10 November 1975
Portugal grants Angola
independence

25 April 1976
First democratic elections since
dictatorship set up in 1928

1990

prestigious Portuguese military academy also reflected this disillusionment: in 1971 only 169 people applied for 550 spaces available.

Increasingly discontented, junior officers in the army felt alienated from the regime's colonial policy and its restrictive censorship at home, which cut Portugal off from the new currents of ideas and fashions in Western Europe and North America in the late 1960s and early 1970s.

Junior army officers formed the Armed Forces Movement (MFA) in 1972 and pressure from the MFA began to influence senior officers as they recognized that the colonial war could not be won and that even after Salazar's death in 1970, his successor, Caetano, showed no sign of turning from the old dictator's policies either in Africa or at home. An impasse had been reached which only a revolution could resolve.

THE "REVOLUTION OF FLOWERS"

In February 1974 two generals, Anastasio Spinola and Costa Gomes protested to the government about the futility of its colonial policy. They were removed from their posts, but the Caetano regime's disinterested response finally compelled MFA members to plot a military coup to "save the nation from the government" as their manifesto put it when they launched their operation to seize government buildings and broadcasting facilities overnight on 24–5 April 1974.

Although ordinary people were surprised by the coup, they swarmed onto the streets of Lisbon and other cities to celebrate the almost bloodless collapse of the dictatorship. Soon the tanks guarding public buildings were covered in flowers, which gave the revolution its popular name as the "revolution of flowers". Soldiers wore carnations and decorated the barrels of their guns with them since within hours the whole repressive system of the old regime had collapsed with hardly any resistance.

Although the monocled General Spinola was a popular hero as the highest-ranking opponent of the old regime and was proclaimed provisional president, in practice much younger officers controlled the emerging new regime.

The speedy success of the coup meant that all sorts of questions about future issues had hardly been thought through. What sort of country should Portugal be now that the dictatorship had collapsed? Would it follow West European models or was it really more like a Third World country, such as Cuba for instance, opting to break with the Western democracies that had hypocritically backed the Portuguese dictatorship as a NATO ally?

One thing was clear – there was no more will to fight colonial wars. Even though Spinola had been a ruthless anti-guerrilla commander in Africa and had hoped to reach a compromise with the liberation movements to halt the war, he accepted the decision to abandon Portugal's African empire in July 1974. The dismantling of Portugal's 400-year-old colonial heritage over the next few months led to a mass flight of hundreds of thousands of colonists and quite a few black collaborators from Angola and Mozambique.

In fact, Portugal had an inflow on a per capita basis about five times larger than the mass migration of *pieds noirs* (French colonists living in Algeria) from Algeria to France in 1962. Absorbing this influx posed huge economic problems for Portugal after 1975; amazingly, it was achieved despite the domestic upheaval at the same time.

In many ways, the revolution against the old regime preceded visible symptoms of social and economic unrest. The repressive apparatus of the Salazar system had kept working class and peasant discontent firmly under control. After the "revolution of flowers", strikes escalated rapidly.

The Junta, or Council of National Salvation that was formed to govern Portugal after 25 April was made up of seven officers and was far from conservative. The military under this Council took control of all political decisions. The courts were subordinated to the military in cases where "counter-revolutionary" crime was alleged. Indeed the degree of military control extended far beyond normal government functions to a whole range of issues – even nominating an army officer to represent Portugal in the Eurovision Song Contest!

Land seizures, especially in southern Portugal in 1974, raised the spectre of the abolition of private property. Although many occupations of landlords' property and factories were probably spontaneous and directed by locals at employers associated with the old regime, the communists and some army officers openly advocated a radical programme of nationalization of land

and many industrial and commercial companies. To some it looked as if the programme associated with the Allende government in Chile, before the coup there, might be achieved in Portugal instead.

WEST CONCERN OVER COMMUNISM

When Communist Party leader, Alvaro Cunhal, returned from exile in the Soviet Union to take up a post in the provisional government in May 1974, Portugal's NATO allies worried. The US was concerned that the revolution would lead to a communist takeover in Portugal. Secretary of State, Henry Kissinger, openly, and the CIA, covertly, pulled all the wires within NATO, of which Portugal had been a member for years, to influence events inside the country.

Americans feared that after April 1974 the Portuguese government would be unable to stop a slide towards more radical positions. Kissinger sourly told Mario Soares, the democratic Socialist leader, "You are a Kerensky. I believe your sincerity but you are naïve." When Soares replied, "I certainly don't want to be a Kerensky," Kissinger said, "Neither did Kerensky." (Alexander Kerensky was the shortlived democratic prime minister of Russia before Lenin seized power in November 1917). But in reality, Soares was winning in Portugal.

Although the communists and their allies had enjoyed a sudden boom after the fall of the dictatorship, most Portuguese did not want to go from one extreme to the other. A couple of generations of near isolation from Western Europe meant that most people were anxious not to lose the chance of greater integration with the European Economic Community whose affluence many had judged at first hand, either as so-called guest workers or students in EEC countries or by seeing EEC tourists in Portugal. A vocal group of intellectuals and radical junior army officers might be infatuated with the Soviet model but ordinary Portuguese looked to improvements in their lives, and rights guaranteed in countries closer to hand.

American and West German money, most notably from the West German Social Democrats and their trade union allies (and less publicly from the CIA), went to Soares's party and his allies. Dislike of West German support for Soares was a factor in the burning down of the West German embassy in Lisbon and reflected the growing alienation felt by many Portuguese who feared leftist activities might alienate the country from West European norms.

THE CENTRE-LEFT WIN THE ELECTIONS

In the elections to a Constituent Assembly on the anniversary of the revolution, the Communists obtained only one out of eight

MFA military troops rejoice after the seizure of government buildings and broadcasting facilities in a bloodless coup, 26 April 1974.

of the votes. The Portuguese Socialist Party gained 38 per cent and the Social Democratic Party got more than one quarter of the votes, giving the centre-left alliance a clear majority in the Constitutional Assembly. Almost 90 per cent of Portuguese adults voted despite a campaign by radical military officers to promote abstention as a way of forestalling a moderate victory. The original MFA manifesto at the time of the revolution had committed the army to holding elections to a constituent assembly within a year. Although these fell on the anniversary of the revolution, this was less symbolic than a sign that the radicals had held off the vote until the last possible date without breaking the promise to hold them.

Despite the high voter turnout and the victory of the centre-left, the left-wing radicals did not renounce their revolutionary ambitions. The Communist Party leader, Cunhal, told the press, "If you think the Socialist Party with its 40 per cent and the Popular Democrats with its 27 per cent constitute the majority… you're a victim of a misunderstanding… the elections have nothing or very little to do with the dynamics of a revolution." Cunhal even promised, "There will be no parliament in Portugal."

The Communist leader's perspective was shared by some radical army officers, but the scale of the election turnout and the left's defeat led many former radicals to accept the legitimacy of the newly elected parliament even when challenged by the Military Revolutionary Council. An attempted backlash by the radical left in the autumn of 1975 collapsed ignominiously, permitting Soares to

shift economic policy even further away from communist-backed nationalization. In the April 1976 general election, votes confirmed the previous year's turnout and the communists were confined to the margins of parliamentary politics.

Another potential obstacle to Portugal's transition to democracy was Franco's Spain next door. Some diehard Salazar supporters had hoped for Spanish intervention to suppress the Portuguese revolution but the elderly Spanish dictator took no action. In September 1975, possibly radical left-wing provocateurs set fire to the Spanish embassy in Lisbon, after the pro-communist premier Colonel Vasco Goncales was removed, but Spain remained passive and the democratic process in Portugal continued.

THE NEW DEMOCRATIC CONSTITUTION

Soares used the shift in power to promote a new constitution that proclaimed classical liberal values rather than the economic and social issues urged by the radical left. However, it was only in 1982 that the residual rights of the military council to interfere in politics were abolished, though in practice the army had withdrawn years before.

Although at the time it looked as if the Portuguese revolution might lead to a radical challenge to West European norms of parliamentary democracy and the market economy, in fact by the early 1980s Portugal had become a model of the transition to democracy for other dictatorial regimes, especially in Latin America.

NATIONAL UPRISINGS

Introduction

"One man's terrorist is another man's freedom fighter." Anonymous

"Nationalism, that magnificent song that made the people rise against their oppressor, stops short, falters, and dies away on the day that independence is proclaimed." Frantz Fanon, black activist

Nationalism has produced at least as great a revolutionary force as any movement based on social or economic discontents. Of course when discontent about the suppression of national identity is combined with socio-economic distress then peculiarly powerful emotive forces may well be released. The struggle for national independence, whether allied to calls for social justice or not, poses ideological challenges to the rebels that lead them down the path to declaring and justifying their call for emancipation or independence.

EARLY REBELS

Early fighters for national rights like the Dutch rebels of the later 16th century or the American revolutionaries in the 1770s often saw themselves as essentially conservative. They believed that new foreign rulers had imposed unjustified novel taxes and other forms of oppression absent in the past. To a great extent their resistance began as a call

to return to some better past, but the logic of resistance drove them to justify their cause. Frequently the nature of the struggle forced rebels to adopt revolutionary conclusions, such as declaring an independent republic in the case of the 16th-century Dutch or the Americans in 1776. Accompanying such declarations of independence were theoretical statements of the right to revolution, which played a big role in those revolutions and in providing an arsenal of ideas and justifications for later, often-unforeseen struggles.

Although opinions varied on the topic, in the 1960s many Americans were dismayed that the Vietnamese had plagiarized the Declaration of Independence and thrown it back in their faces.

FREQUENTLY VIOLENT STRUGGLES

Because nationalism is almost invariably the ideology encompassing a struggle to control a territory as well as liberate a people, a revolution of national liberation usually involves violence. After all, the colonial power or minority group ruling the state has very often acquired its power by force and needs to keep it by the ever-present threat of force. The spiral of violence witnessed in places as diverse as Algeria, Angola, or America helps to create national identity and solidarity.

NON-VIOLENT RESISTANCE

Sometimes nationalisms have achieved their goals by peaceful means. Mahatma Gandhi's "Quit India Movement" developed an unprecedented array of non-violent means of passive resistance to undermine British imperial rule over India by 1947. However, as Gandhi was the first to admit, non-violence only worked against certain opponents. The British Raj fancied itself as a civilizing force bringing the rule of law and respect for individual rights to India. Although on occasions the British used savage force to suppress protesting crowds (as in the Massacre at Amritsar in 1919), their very ideology of empire made it inconceivable for them to use the kind of sustained brutality needed to break the spirit and cohesion of a

A mural by Willie Bester pays homage to Steve Biko, the political activist and anti-apartheid martyr who advocated complete emancipation for black South Africans.

movement like Gandhi's. Numbers counted too, of course. To hold down India's vast population was beyond Britain's resources, certainly after the strain of World War II, during which the empire's appeal had soured for those who had elected a new Labour government on the eve of victory over Japan.

The largely non-violent anti-apartheid struggle in South Africa before 1994 was based on the recognition that the black majority lacked the weapons to force the white minority to concede one person one vote. Although some guerrilla activity occurred in the last 30 years of apartheid, the greatest pressure on the regime came from unarmed protest (which faced violence from the white authorities) and international pressure for change through sanctions and boycotts in countries that South Africa liked to think of as friends.

THE ROLE OF PUBLIC OPINION

The role of international sympathy in the success of national liberation movements is an easily forgotten factor. Sometimes rival great powers to the colonial ruler back the rebels out of Machiavellian calculations of strategic advantage, such as when France helped the Americans against Great Britain after 1777, but frequently public opinion is an independent actor, even when pushing for government action. For instance, the struggle for Greek independence in the 1820s would have been still more difficult if the memory of classical Greece was not such a strong one among West European educated elites

who identified modern Greeks fighting the Turks with the ancient Greeks battling the Persian despot Xerxes. (Of course, critics of Western "orientalist" prejudices could not help noting that some freedom fighters, like the Greeks, were viewed more sympathetically because of their Christianity and ancient culture than more alien peoples who lacked an easy identifying tag for Western audiences.)

Even the French army found that new media technologies like the transistor radio and instant reports of atrocities undermined domestic support for their war to keep Algeria under French control (1954–62). The role of the media in providing graphic news reports and harrowing images of war from Vietnam in the 1960s and 1970s is much debated but there can be little doubt that the anti-war movement on US university campuses and in many parts of North America would never have become so vocal and intense if television pictures of what was happening in South East Asia after 1965, and of the US military role, had not existed.

THE LOGIC OF REVOLUTION

National liberation movements have repeatedly demonstrated the fallibility of conventional notions of the balance of power and the irresistibility of apparently overwhelming force. Radical writer Tariq Ali noted about Vietnam after the collapse of the American-sponsored South Vietnamese regime in 1975, "The logic of war dictated that the Americans should win, but this logic had been superseded by one superior and infinitely more powerful: the logic of revolution." Whether it was an irreducible ideological commitment on the part of the anti-American Vietnamese fighters, or what some commentators have called a "territorial imperative" that made them fight so much more tenaciously for their own soil than the GIs from the other side of the Pacific, what became clear was that even destructive firepower surpassing the bomb loads dropped during the whole of World War II was not enough to defeat an enemy prepared to sacrifice so much.

It was reported at the time that though the North Vietnamese leaders, Ho Chi Minh and General Giap, were awed in 1967 by the vast destructive might of the Pentagon, they breathed a sigh of relief when they heard the US Secretary of Defense say his purpose was to inflict an "unacceptable" level of casualties on them. They realized that the Americans had a limit to how many US soldiers they would sacrifice, and Ho Chi Minh and Giap guessed it was a lower limit than theirs.

TRIBAL LOYALTY

Not every national liberation struggle is supported by the populace. In some societies an ethnic religious group may dislike their rulers or the local majority, but can be ambivalent about violence as a means of liberation. In both contemporary Spain's northern Basque country and Britain's Northern Ireland, many want self-government or independence and are suspicious of what they see as a foreign or colonial central government. However, the number who actively support terrorist groups like the Basque ETA movement or the various IRA groups in Northern Ireland is a much smaller percentage than the nationalist element in the population at large. The problem for even democratic countries like Spain or Britain, is that although many ordinary citizens would not engage in the "liberation struggle" or terrorism, they also would not inform on those who did. This unwillingness to cooperate with police is not just based on fear of reprisals but rather on the powerful residue of shared identity with the outlawed groups who oppose the state.

Whether dismissed as "tribalism" or praised as "patriotism", the strength of group identities is one of the key underlying factors in the resurgence of national liberation movements. Those who dismiss such identities are oblivious to their own tribal loyalty, which seems unquestionably normal.

DISAPPEARING COLONIAL RULE

Although colonial rule has largely disappeared across the world and the UN has wound up its anti-colonial committee, there are still many minorities in states who resent their status. At the same time the force of economic and technological globalization is creating new haves and have-nots, which could easily spawn future liberation movements with a pronounced nationalist and anti-capitalist bias.

Greece 1820s

The Greek war of liberation against Ottoman Turkish rule in the 1820s brought together national liberation with social revolution as centuries-old Turkish dominion was overthrown. However, at the start of the 19th century, with the Greek-speaking population of south-eastern Europe scattered and divided, it was far from obvious that a successful revolt could occur.

Educated Western Europeans still associated Greece with the classical literature of Athens and the legends of Homer, however romantic. But the sad reality was that the Ottoman Turkish conquest of the Greek-speaking Byzantine Empire 350 years earlier, in 1453, had marked the extinction of classical Greek society. Since that time, Christian Greeks seemed condemned to second-class status as subjects of the Muslim Turkish sultan, paying higher taxes and subject to compulsory labour, amongst other penalties.

Greek-speaking Christians were scattered across much of the Ottoman Empire not just in the ancient heartland but across the Aegean in Asia Minor and along the coast of the Black Sea. Centuries of suppression gave way to hopes of liberation as Ottoman power decayed in the 18th century and Western states like France and Britain, along with the emerging Russian empire, began to encroach on its territories.

The possibility of foreign aid raised hopes for independence but never appeared – most recently in 1770 when the Greek rebels expected help from Catherine the Great's Russia but were disappointed when she made territorial gains for Russia and then left them to their fate. However, the impact of the French Revolution in destabilizing the Eastern Mediterranean both politically and ideologically was much more important. Whereas the Russian Empire was primarily concerned with its own territorial expansion, the French revolutionary armies brought printing presses and opened schools on Corfu, and spread the ideas of liberty and equality as well as French power.

The occupation of Corfu and the other Ionian Islands by first the French republic in 1797 and then as a republic outside the Ottoman empire under British control after 1815 was an example close to home of how Greeks could break free of Turkish rule, especially with foreign aid. Although first the French then the British occupiers of the Ionian Islands were foreigners, as Christians with a classical education they treated the

Greeks in a wholly different way from the Turks and encouraged self-government.

Not all Greeks favoured independence. In Constantinople itself there was a significant Greek presence in the sultan's bureaucracy and a loyal Greek commanded his fleet throughout the independence war. However, the Turks tended to take reprisals against loyal Greeks for rebel actions and in doing so, succeeded in alienating many of them.

AN INTELLECTUAL RENAISSANCE

The most important Greek institution was the Orthodox Church and by 1800 it was experiencing a revival after generations of subjection to the sultanate. Although leadership of the church in Constantinople remained in the hands of frequently corrupt and servile men, many ordinary clergy in Greece were promoting a renaissance of their ancient church's intellectual traditions. The clergy's educational level improved and revived interest in the pre-Ottoman Byzantine period, which helped reignite Greek national pride, as did a recovered awareness of ancient Greece's centrality to

The widely recognized Parthenon was one of many symbols that Western thinkers associated with classical Greece and the struggle for Greek independence.

		April 1828 War breaks out between Turkey and Russia		
February 1822 *Ali Pasha defeated and murdered*	**May 1827** *Greeks elect ex-Russian foreign minister, Kapodistrias, president*		**1832** *Convention of London sets up monarchy in Greece*	**May 1844** *Liberal constitution*

| **13 January 1822** *Greek independence and first constitution proclaimed* | **18 April 1824** *Lord Byron dies of fever at Missolonghi* | **1830** **20 October 1827** *Anglo-French-Russian fleet defeats Turks at Navarino* | **9 October 1831** *Kapodistrias assassinated at Nafplion* | **February 1833** *King Otto arrives in Greece* |

Western culture, which foreign travellers like Byron brought to Greece.

The combined influence of new ideas from France and the resurgence of Greek Orthodoxy stimulated rebellion. But there were also many socio-economic causes. In much of the southern Balkans, Greeks, like other Christians, lived disadvantaged lives compared with Muslims. Although there were some Christian landowners, their property was insecure and heavily taxed. The bulk of landless peasants were even worse off.

Poverty and anger with Turkish rule bred rebel gangs who robbed passers-by in the rough terrain. The klephts, the Greek bandits, were Robin Hood figures who combined robbery with patriotism. One of the most famous klephts, Theodoros Kolokotronis, began as a bandit but worked his way up to Ottoman-sponsored policeman (armatolos) and eventually to the illustrious position of patriotic general. Despite his colourful biography, Kolokotronis was far from just a Greek bandit on the make. He took an interest in foreign affairs, especially the impact of the French Revolution, and in his memoirs argued, "The French Revolution and the doings of Napoleon opened the eyes of the world."

One source of links with the West was the important Greek mercantile class that increasingly favoured independence. It provided money and connections in the West that helped to promote the cause abroad.

Missolonghi, the noted Greek city where the poet, Lord Byron, died of malaria, was also the subject of Eugene Delacroix's painting, Greece on the ruins of Missolonghi.

THE FIGHT FOR INDEPENDENCE

The war of independence in 1821 broke out in two very different theatres. In the north, the pro-independence "Philiki Etairia" or "Friendly Society" had been founded in 1814 by the Greek community in the Black Sea port of Odessa, then in the Russian Empire. The society invaded Turkish-controlled

Romania in the hope of stimulating a rebellion among the Greek communities there. The society's aim was the "liberation of the Motherland", which meant anywhere where Greeks lived. The Friendly Society had Russian backing to destabilize their traditional rival, the sultan. Many of its early members, like its leader Alexander Ypsilantis, had served in the Russian Army during the Napoleonic Wars. His invasion quickly ended in fiasco because the local Romanians disliked their Greek neighbours (and tax collectors) more than the Turks.

Further south, the sultan had decided to remove a subject who threatened his regime, Ali Pasha of Ionanina in north-west Greece. Ostensibly the sultan's governor in north-western Greece and southern Albania, Ali Pasha, had become a powerful independent ruler who engaged in diplomacy with the European Great Powers, including Britain and France. He was deeply influenced by the career of Napoleon and aspired to be what Byron called a "Muslim Bonaparte". Rather than face execution, Ali Pasha rebelled. His resistance drew off Turkish troops, allowing the Greek revolt to succeed further south. For the first time in 400 years, large parts of Morea and the Peloponnese in southern Greece achieved freedom from Turkish rule. In what would now be called "ethnic cleansing", Greeks forcibly drove Turks from their homes.

The bitterly fought war drew Western idealists, like the poet Byron, to the Greek side, which seemed to revive ancient Greek republicanism with the independence constitution of 1822. More important aid came from the Great Powers, who were anxious to avoid a Turkish victory that might mark the start of an Ottoman revival. An Anglo-French-Russian fleet posed a problem for both Greeks and Turks because of their declared neutrality. Nevertheless, the fleet attacked a Turkish-Egyptian fleet that challenged European naval supremacy and destroyed it at Navarino in October 1827. The vigorous Turkish-Egyptian army on Greek soil was cut off and the prospect of a revived Muslim great power stymied. This effectively led to Greek independence as the sultan could not hope to fight both the rebels and the Great Powers and win.

The new Greek republic was short-lived. Its first president was the ex-Russian diplomat, Ioannis Kapodistrias, whose ambitions to establish a modern centralized state brought him into conflict with rural warlords who had fought the Turks, and a disgruntled clan, which murdered him. The Great Powers established a monarchy without consulting the Greeks on their choice. It was not the last time Greek's government was decided by outsiders. The problem was that post-independence Greece had a type of Western European constitutional system grafted onto a still traditional and clannish society where liberal labels were plastered over ancient loyalties and enmities without resolving them. The Greek War of Independence was the first successful European war of liberation. Debates about whether it achieved its ideals have haunted Greece since.

Europe 1848

More than a generation after the defeat of Napoleon in 1815, key figures from among his conquerors like the Chancellor of the Austrian Empire, Clemens von Metternich, were still in power at the start of 1848. Such men had suppressed the demands for constitutional rights and the abolition of the feudal order not only in their own states but also across Europe. The Holy Alliance led by Austria, Russia, and Prussia established in 1815 had intervened to quell revolutionary aspirations in Italy, Spain, Germany, and Poland as well as at home.

NEW IDEAS TOPPLE THE OLD ORDER

By the beginning of 1848, the reign of elderly statesmen and their inadequate hereditary monarchs was beginning to wobble. Industrialization and the development of railways carrying cheap products and new ideas began undermining the old order. Even the weather conspired against the reactionary order as cold and rain wrought havoc with harvests in what became known as the "Hungry Forties".

Late in 1847, two obscure German revolutionaries in French exile, Karl Marx and Friedrich Engels, published their *Communist Manifesto* warning that "a spectre is haunting Europe – the spectre of communism." Although they were right to sense that the new industrial working class toiling in grim factories and the increasingly unemployed pre-industrial handicraft workers across Europe were boiling with discontent, an even more formidable revolutionary movement was threatening the old order: nationalism. Combined with the discontent of the new commercial entrepreneurs and allied groups, like lawyers, who did well out of industrialization but were denied political rights, the forces of working-class unrest and nationalist ambitions created broad coalitions that suddenly erupted in revolution in early 1848, revealing how shallow support for the monarchical order had become.

CONSTITUTIONAL RIGHTS DEMANDED

Starting in southern Italy and Sicily in January 1848, and spreading rapidly northwards to Austrian-controlled Milan and into France, crowds denouncing economic injustices and demanding constitutional rights took their rulers by surprise. The biggest upheavals seemed to require the least effort. On 24

December 1847 *Karl Marx and Friedrich Engels publish their* Communist Manifesto

22 February 1848 *Uprising against Louis Philippe begins in Paris*

13 March 1848 *Metternich flees Vienna into exile in London*

18 March 1848 *Revolution begins in Berlin*

22 March 1848 *Restoration of Venetian republic proclaimed*

1848

3 January 1848 *Uprising against Austrian rule begins in Milan*

25 February 1848 *Second French republic proclaimed*

15 March 1848 *Hungarian parliament passes March Laws*

18–22 March 1848 *Street-fighting drives Austrian Army out of Milan*

29 March 1848 *King of Prussia appoints liberal ministers*

February, after two days of street protests in Paris, the French king, Louis Philippe, fled into exile to England and the people declared a republic. On 13 March, Metternich himself fled in panic from Vienna and Emperor Ferdinand conceded a government composed of liberal ministers. When news of Metternich's fall reached Berlin on 18 March, the king of Prussia faced huge demonstrations calling for constitutional government. In Austrian-ruled Hungary the previously supine parliament passed laws inspired by the liberal

A painting by Eugene Hagenauer depicts one of the many volatile events in 1848: The burning of the Chateau d'Eau at the Palais-Royal, 24 February 1848.

nationalist, Lajos Kossuth, reasserting self-government and reducing the Emperor Ferdinand to a constitutional monarch. And at decisive moments the political system was paralyzed by both Ferdinand of Austria and Frederick William IV of Prussia's indecision.

Almost everywhere the upheaval had been achieved with minimal bloodshed. Concessions seemed to have been granted at the asking by crowds in the streets. The

23 April 1848 *First democratic elections to National Assembly in France*

27 June 1848 *General Cavaignac suppresses French rebellion*

10 December 1848 *Louis Napoleon Bonaparte elected president of France*

13 April 1849 *Kossuth declared regent of Hungary – fall of Habsburgs*

5–9 May 1849 *Prussian troops suppress the revolution in Dresden, Saxony*

18 May 1848 *Frankfurt parliament opens*

5 December 1848 *Dissolution of Prussian Constituent Assembly*

1849

March 1849 *King of Prussia rejects Frankfurt parliament's offer of German crown*

21 April 1849 *Dissolution of Frankfurt parliament*

speed of change was illusory, however; key institutions of the old order, especially the army, remained unreformed across Europe.

While liberal lawyers set about drafting new constitutions, enshrining the principles of human rights and democratic government that so many people had aspired to since 1789, disgruntled army officers set about plotting the reversal of the revolutions.

REVOLUTIONARIES COME TO POWER

Both in France and across the diverse states making up the German confederation, democratic elections were held for the first time in the spring of 1848. Radical democrats who had been at the forefront of the street demonstrations in February and March were disappointed to discover that the people still deferred to their betters or the clergy and voted accordingly.

In France, a huge majority voted for conservative, even monarchist candidates. The rural population outnumbered the radical towns and resented early social benefits granted to the unemployed by the republic's provisional government at the expense of taxes on the peasantry.

The new parliamentary majority immediately abolished the dole, offering the unemployed the unappetizing choice of going to Algeria as settlers, joining the army, or living in penury. Revolt broke out in Paris in June 1848, but the new government relied on rural troops to quell the rebels savagely.

This cartoon, entitled The Thin End of the Wedge, *shows Napoleon III and appeared at the time he proposed his candidacy for president of the new Second Republic.*

Ironically, General Cavaignac did for the republic what no reactionary general had been able to do for a monarch – drown popular revolution in blood.

The beneficiary of the popular revulsion at Cavaignac's brutality was Napoleon I's nephew, Louis Napoleon Bonaparte, who easily defeated Cavaignac in the French presidential election on 10 December 1848. Louis Napoleon's victory marked the beginning of the end of the French republic. Determined to restore his uncle's empire, Louis Napoleon used his popular mandate to undermine the parliamentarians in the National Assembly. After so much upheaval most French were prepared to accept their president as dictator and then emperor when on 2 December 1851, his troops dispersed the National Assembly and suppressed the few left-wing demonstrators.

French reactionaries' success emboldened their Central European counterparts. Playing on resentments between peasant troops and urban revolutionaries, generals used force to suppress both the liberals demanding constitutional changes and the workers with their economic grievances.

NATIONALISM AND INTOLERANCE SURGE

It was not only town and country that were at odds. The year 1848 had seen an upsurge in nationalism as not only Germans and Italians called for the unification of their divided peoples but also the Slav nationalities of Europe, like the Czechs and Poles, along with the Hungarians, demanded their own states. Tragically, the achievement of national sovereignty, at least by the Germans, came at the expense of denying the rights of others, like the Czechs or Poles who lived on land claimed by the German "democrats" at the national parliament in Frankfurt.

To assert their national rights, the short-sighted German democrats asked the king of Prussia to send his army to force Danes in the north and Poles in the province of Posen to remain in Germany. Defeating Germany's national enemies, their generals then turned them on the naïve liberals, who had called them out in the first place. Meanwhile divisions arose between supporters of industrialization and property rights and more radical groups, opening the door to defeat by professional soldiers.

The most successful 1848 revolution was in Hungary, at least at first. There Metternich's fall led to the overthrow of the whole Austrian system of domination. A new constitutional order was established. However, the Hungarian liberals were also nationalists and intolerant of their own minorities: Romanian, Serbian, and Slovak who wanted self-rule against "liberal" Budapest. The Hungarian army fought valiantly and required the intervention of a 250,000-strong Russian army to force them to surrender to Austria in August 1849.

Although the liberal and nationalist revolutions all seemed to have collapsed by the end of 1849 they left a legacy of limited reforms and the memory of brief freedoms to stir future unrest.

Ireland 1916–22

The Easter Uprising against British rule in Ireland in 1916 set in train the violent events leading to the establishment of an independent Ireland in 1922. This was the culminating episode in a long and unhappy history of British domination over Ireland which started 1172 when Norman knights crossed the Irish Sea to conquer the country.

A KINGDOM DIVIDED

In 1801, the British Parliament intended to incorporate largely Catholic Ireland into the mainly Protestant United Kingdom. However, over the coming century, religious differences and unexpected events repeatedly drove the countries apart.

Terrible famine, caused by potato blight in 1845–6, forced mass emigration abroad, to England or America. The Irish blamed insufficient British relief efforts on the hard-hearted indifference of London politicians rather than their incapacity to grasp the scale of the problem and organize supplies quickly.

Rural discontent boiled up, with violent attacks on landlords, boycotts, and increasing use of the extensions of voting rights in the later 19th century to support Irish nationalist candidates for the British Parliament.

In 1912 the Irish National Parties' 72 MPs held the balance of power in the British Parliament and the ruling Liberal Party agreed to offer Home Rule to Ireland in return for their support. This would have let Ireland run its own internal affairs but retain the British king as its head of state, with foreign and defence policy still decided in London. However, the Protestant minority in the six northern counties of Ulster declared their bitter opposition to leaving the Union. Bent on civil war, both Nationalists and Ulster Unionists formed volunteer forces until another much greater war broke out in August 1914 between Britain and Germany.

As far back as the English Civil War in the 1640s, Irish rebels had hoped to overthrow English rule while London was preoccupied overseas. The First World War offered a great opportunity to the radical Irish nationalists who had formed their own fringe party, Sinn Fein ("Ourselves Alone") in 1907. Although implementation of the Home Rule Bill's was to be suspended during the war, the Irish National Party encouraged Irish Catholics to join the British Army. Thousands enlisted (many to escape unemployment), but most refused to fight abroad. Hoping to trigger an unsuppressible nationwide revolt,

1 January 1801 Act of Union merges Ireland into the United Kingdom

1907 Sinn Fein formed

4 August 1914 War breaks out with Germany and Home Rule suspended

1900

1845–6 Potato famine ravages rural Ireland

1910

1912–14 British Parliament passes Irish Home Rule Bill

radicals plotted an uprising while millions of British troops fought on the Western Front. Some radicals abroad sought military aid from the Germans, a treasonous offence, but Germany could offer no aid.

BLOODSHED RADICALIZES THE IRISH

Sinn Fein ideologists, like Padraig Pearse, developed a mystical ideology of Ireland, as a land to be redeemed by a "blood sacrifice" of willing martyrs, and formed an Irish Republican Army (IRA). Despite lack of German support and lukewarm backing from within Ireland, on Easter Monday Pearse and his comrades occupied central Dublin, proclaiming an Irish Republic at their temporary headquarters, the Post Office, in Sackville Street. About 1,600 volunteers occupied a collection of buildings across Dublin, though administrative centres, like the castle, were not seized.

British troops rushed to suppress the rebellion in five days of bitter fighting. Initially, Dubliners reacted unsympathetically to the surrendering volunteers, whose uprising had led to 318 civilian deaths against only 64 rebels and had wrecked much of the city. But the British military commander gave the rebels as much bloody propaganda as they could have asked for. He ordered 15 rebel leaders shot, making them instant martyrs. Under martial law 3,500 people were arrested but many had nothing to do with the revolt. To the British, harsh measures were justified – the rebels had betrayed them, in effect aiding Germany. But Pearse's intuition about "blood sacrifice" proved right in radicalizing the Irish people.

The British government worsened matters by exempting the six counties of Ulster from the suspended Home Rule provisions. This decision shattered support for the moderate Irish Nationalist leader, John Redmond, who had cooperated with the British war effort, and Sinn Fein began to gain support as the real exponents of Irish self-government. By 1918, Sinn Fein candidates regularly won by-elections in once-safe Irish National Party seats. Their supporters were about 250,000 strong in 1,200 Sinn Fein clubs across Ireland. In July 1917 the surviving leader of the Easter Uprising, Eammon De Valera, who avoided execution because of his US passport, won a landslide election in East Clare on an openly republican platform.

In April 1918 the world war intensified and the British government extended wartime conscription to Ireland. This re-galvanized the radical volunteers who wanted no part of England's war. It also gave Sinn Fein an issue to bash the National Party with, since its leaders had supported voluntary service in the British Army and were now backtracking when more sacrifices were demanded by London. In turn, the British

29 April 1916 Surviving rebels surrender

11 July 1921 Truce between British and Irish forces

16 June 1922 Irish Free State general election – women given the vote

24 April 1916 Irish Republic proclaimed – Easter Rising begins

1920

21 January 1919 Sinn Fein MPs assemble in Dublin as Dail Eireann

6 December 1921 Anglo-Irish Treaty defines status of Irish Free State

24 May 1923 Ceasefire: IRA tells its men to dump weapons

1930

authorities accused Sinn Fein of supporting a German plot to disrupt the war effort (like Lenin's Bolsheviks in Russia the year earlier) and made a wave of arrests, angering many.

A KINGDOM DIVIDED

A snap British general election in December, and held in Ireland, followed the sudden end of the First World War in November 1918. While the Unionist Coalition won a huge majority elsewhere in Britain, in Ireland Sinn Fein won 73 seats or 65 per cent of the vote outside Ulster. London and Dublin were now on a collision course as Sinn Fein MPs refused to take their seats in the Westminster Parliament and formed their own Dail Eireann in Dublin as the Parliament of an unrecognized Irish Republic in January 1919. Meanwhile IRA supporters of Sinn Fein began bombing and assassinating British authorities and Catholic "collaborators" with the British. The great bulk of policemen, postmen, and local officials were Catholics. The IRA's terrorism intimidated many of them and their families out of British service.

The British enlisted ex-servicemen from the British wartime to fight the IRA. These so-called "Black and Tans" (named because of their distinctive uniforms) lacked local knowledge and frequently responded to IRA attacks with atrocities of their own, alienating ordinary Irish people and escalating the violence. About 17,000 Royal Irish Constabulary men and Black-and-Tans fought around 5,000 IRA men in an increasingly savage war on both sides.

The two key Republican figures were Eammon De Valera and Michael Collins, both survivors of the Easter Rising. De Valera raised more than $5 million from fellow Irish Americans, which gave Sinn Fein a huge advantage in the propaganda rivalry with the old Irish National Party and paid for many weapons. Collins was the key military organizer of the movement and terrorizer of the British forces and their sympathizers.

Although both De Valera and Collins seemed to be unbending nationalists, Collins was prepared to compromise to end the fighting. Recognizing that the Protestant Unionists of Ulster would not accept incorporation into a Sinn Fein-dominated south, Collins bargained with the British over self-government for 26 counties of Ireland.

Collins met the arch-unionists, including Winston Churchill, and reached a compromise. Twenty-six of Ireland's 32 counties were to get independence with a government in Dublin, with the British king remaining nominal head of state and the Royal Navy keeping access to Ireland's key ports. Northern Ireland, however, would have a separate, Unionist-dominated government and would remain part of the UK. Many Irish Republicans felt betrayed by the compromise, which destroyed their dreams of an all-Ireland Republic. A vicious civil war ensued.

De Valera led the rejectionist wing of the IRA, turning on former comrades who sold out to the British, including Michael Collins, who was murdered in a surprise attack by his former comrades. But the IRA's hard-line approach alienated many supporters.

Members of the Irish Republican Army surrender after the Easter uprising of 1916, in a scene from the 1996 film Michael Collins.

By the spring of 1923 De Valera's men were losing the civil war and called a cease-fire. The Free Staters had lost 800 men. The IRA's losses were certainly higher, with hundreds of civilians caught in the crossfire.

Even when the IRA accepted the ceasefire at the end of May 1923, it refused to give up its arms, and "dumped" them where they could be retrieved for future struggles. It was the start of a long IRA tradition of halting the armed struggle but never disarming until their goal of a united all-Ireland republic was achieved. Although an Irish Republic and withdrawal from the British Commonwealth was declared in 1948, Ulster remained troubled, even after De Valera's death in 1975.

By the late 1960s the second-class status of Catholics in Protestant-ruled Northern Ireland sparked civil rights protests and a terrorist campaign by a reinvigorated IRA. Thirty years of mutual terror and counter-terrorism led to a peace process in the late 1990s, between the British government and Protestant leaders, and nationalist politicians and the political wing of the IRA. Although a ceasefire was agreed, full disarmament by either side failed to materialize, leaving Protestants and Catholics to view each other with suspicion.

Vietnam 1945–75

Japanese occupation of French Indo-China in 1940 shattered the old colonial system as it did elsewhere in Asia. Resistance movements against Japanese rule swelled, but freedom fighters wanted complete independence not the return of European colonial masters. The collapse of Japanese power in August 1945, with the dropping of the Atomic Bomb, created a vacuum of control in Vietnam.

Ho Chi Minh, the French-educated Vietnamese communist, organized guerrilla resistance, known as the Vietminh, against Japanese occupation and, like Mao in China, saw no reason to stop his liberation struggle in August 1945 when France tried to restore its control and even impudently asked the Japanese troops to remain until French soldiers arrived. Ho Chi Minh anticipated that Paris would not agree to Vietnamese independence. The American Declaration of Independence was the model for his own proclamation on 2 September 1945, but this cut little ice with post-war Washington. The new Truman Administration backed the restoration of French imperial control to avoid any risk of a communist takeover.

France organized local forces to oppose the Vietminh and promoted the traditional Emperor, Bao Dao, as a kind of local leader, but it was clear to all involved that France intended to preserve control. As a result Vietnamese nationalists tended to drift to the Vietminh side. French savagery, like the bombardment of the port of Haiphong in April 1946, which killed 6,000 people, increasingly alienated the Vietnamese.

As early as 1946, Ho Chi Minh perceptively recognized that France could not afford a prolonged conflict when he told a French interviewer: "You will kill 10 of our men, but we will kill one of yours and it is you who will end by wearing yourselves out." The fact that France could not risk sending conscripts to fight in Vietnam showed how shallow Paris felt support for the reconquest of Vietnam was. Instead France relied on professionals and foreign legionaries, many of them with a dubious past in Nazi Europe before 1945.

FRENCH FALL AT DIEN BIEN PHU

Recognizing that even 165,000 soldiers were not enough to hold down Vietnam, like many colonial masters convinced of their technical superiority, the French commanders were anxious to force the guerrillas out into an open battle that could be decisively won.

June 1940 Japan occupies French Indo-China

21 November 1953 French paratroops set up base at Dien Bien Phu

20 July 1954 Geneva Agreement sets up independence in Vietnam and South-east Asia

November 1963 Assassination of President Diem by CIA-backed generals

1945

2 September 1945 Ho Chi Minh proclaims Vietnamese independence

13 March–7 May 1954 Siege of Dien Bien Phu

26 October 1955 The Republic of (South) Vietnam proclaimed

1960

2 August 1964 Gulf of Tonkin incident used to justify US entry into war

Bien Phu near the Laotian border, drawing the opposition leader, General Giap, into a pitched battle in March 1954.

Despite terrible conditions in the jungle, Giap's men and coolies dragged heavy weapons over the mountains, surrounded the French base with artillery platforms, and cut off its supply chain by bombarding the airstrips that linked Dien Bien Phu to Hanoi. The French garrison fought with great courage but could not break the siege despite sacrificing thousands of lives. The survivors finally surrendered on 7 May 1954.

The fall of Dien Bien Phu shattered French willingness to carry on the fight, but America stepped in. Washington switched subsidies from the French Army in Vietnam to a Saigon-based regime in the south of the country in opposition to Ho Chi Minh's government in the northern capital, Hanoi.

French soldiers make their way thtough a swamp in the region of Cau Ngam Donmau in South Vietnam, in the direction of a Vietminh enclave, in November 1950.

Once China fell to Mao's communists and then the Korean War broke out in 1950, France presented its Vietnam War as a crusade against communism and looked to staunchly democratic America for support. Washington willingly supplied cash and supplies to fund the war but left the fighting to the French. In 1954, foolishly, the new French commander, Navarre, provoked a showdown in the remote valley base of Dien

THE GENEVA AGREEMENT

Although the Geneva Agreement in July 1954, which sealed the French withdrawal, had stipulated a united Vietnam after elections, in practice the 17th parallel of latitude became the dividing line between a communist North and a Western-backed South Vietnam.

Despite promises to hold elections throughout Vietnam as part of the Geneva deal, the pro-American South reneged on

29 January 1968 *Tet Offensive – lasts until 25 February 1968*

4 May 1970 *Four anti-war protesters shot dead at Kent State University, Ohio*

30 April 1975 *Saigon falls to North Vietnam – renamed Ho Chi Minh City*

3 September 1969 *eath of Ho Chi Minh*

April 1970 *US forces invade Cambodia*

1975

27 January 1973 *Paris Agreement signed to end conflict*

7 January 1979 *Vietnamese Army captures Phnom Penh and forces Pol Pot underground*

1990

the deal, backed by the Eisenhower Administration. Americans feared that after defeating France Ho Chi Minh's communists would sweep to victory across Vietnam.

US BACK A COUP IN THE SOUTH

Eisenhower's Administration hoped to buy time to establish an indigenous anti-communist regime in the South, but found itself steadily drawn into the conflict as the guerrilla movement in the South, the Vietcong, became ever more dangerous to the pro-Western Saigon regime.

First Eisenhower, and later President Kennedy, sent in advisers and military specialists to assess the situation and provide guidance. By the time of Kennedy's assassination – unbeknown to the US public – 30,000 US personnel were in fact running the war in the South. The Americans also controlled the politics of the South. Deciding that their protégé, President Diem, was too corrupt to build a genuine following, the Americans endorsed a military coup, which led to his murder only days before Kennedy's assassination in November 1963.

Instead of stabilizing the South, the murder of Diem led to a flurry of coups and counter-coups enabling the rebel stronghold in the south, Vietcong, to extend its "liberated

In the continuous struggle for liberation from foreign rule, Vietminh soldiers engage in reconnaissance missions to the north of Dien Bien Phu.

areas". Although France had not been able to hold Vietnam with 165,000 professional troops, President Johnson was determined not to be "the first US president to lose a war" and he flooded the South with 550,000 GIs by 1968. Yet more American troops and advanced US technology proved no more successful at suppressing the Vietcong. The Americans could sweep through territory and annihilate open resistance but sniping, booby-traps, and ambushes sapped morale. Most of the GIs were drafted and saw little reason to fight for people they either did not understand or even despised.

Worse still, from the point of view of creating a viable South Vietnam, the US forces relegated the South Vietnamese to auxiliaries in their campaign. It became an American war fought the American way, using vast firepower from planes and artillery to strike at Vietcong forces, or at areas thought to be housing them, despite terrible collateral civilian losses.

Combined with the US policy of concentrating peasants in "protected hamlets", the bombing shattered communities and caused bitter resentment among Vietnamese peasants. US troops had insuperable difficulties distinguishing peasants from Vietcong rebels, leading to many tragedies. Ho Chi Minh noted that his guerrillas moved among the peasants "like fish in the sea".

THE TET OFFENSIVE

The success of guerrilla warfare induced over-confidence in General Giap, who decided to risk a general insurrection and conventional attack timed to coincide with the Tet Festival marking the New Year at the end of January 1968. In fact, the Tet Offensive resulted in devastating losses for the Vietcong and North Vietnamese regulars. But the fact that it had been launched only weeks after American generals had assured reporters that such an attack was impossible meant that the US public saw only a major setback for US policy. After all, even the American embassy in Saigon had come under direct attack. President Johnson drew personal conclusions from Tet and announced that he would not be running for another term in office.

Johnson's eventual successor, Richard Nixon, ran for election as the man who would bring peace but would act firmly. In reality, Nixon tried to force Hanoi to compromise by extending the war. Massive bombing raids of the North itself and an invasion of Cambodia in 1970, intended to cut the so-called Ho Chi Minh Trail bringing supplies and troops from North Vietnam, caused huge protests in the United States because Nixon had promised to wind the war down in his presidential campaign. His actions did more to destabilize Cambodia than persuade the communists to give up the war. Nixon began to wind down US involvement on the ground in South Vietnam, though the US air force continued to play a major role, for instance, in halting another major North Vietnamese offensive in 1972.

Peace negotiations had been conducted between the Americans and North

Vietnamese since Johnson's presidency, but eventually in Paris in January 1973 both the Americans and their South Vietnamese allies agreed to a deal with North Vietnam and the Vietcong. In essence the Paris Agreement acknowledged the stalemate, allowing each side to continue controlling whatever territory it occupied and leaving the timetable for elections leading to reunification open. However, the American troops' withdrawal and Nixon's growing difficulties over Watergate meant that Hanoi could wait confidently for the South Vietnamese to be left to defend themselves, which they could not hope to manage for any extended length of time.

After the last US troops were withdrawn in 1973, the American public was happy to turn its back on what had become a national nightmare for Americans. The Watergate controversy forced Nixon's resignation and shifted American politics briefly to the left. The new US majority had little sympathy for the South Vietnamese leader, ex-general turned president, Nyugen van Thieu, who was widely regarded as the head of a corrupt regime. The US Congress even cut off arms supplies to its former allies in Saigon. The war had stopped only for the Americans, it was about to enter its decisive phase for the Vietnamese.

Without US arms supplies, air support, and advice on the ground the South Vietnamese Army was hopelessly ill prepared to face the final North Vietnamese offensive in spring 1975. Thieu's regime remained as corrupt and complacent as before, only now without

an American ace to back it. Abandoned by the Americans, the South Vietnamese troops melted away as the North launched an all-out offensive. Scenes of panic reminiscent of the fall of Shanghai in 1949 were repeated in Saigon as thousands of desperate people tried to clamber aboard helicopters evacuating the lucky few to US ships offshore. The debacle was complete as was the victory of peasant communists over Western-backed but unpopular local elites.

KHMER ROUGE ATTACKS PHNOM PENH

At the same time, the Khmer Rouge emerged from the jungle to launch a final assault on the Phnom Penh regime. Its forces too were soon in retreat, but had even less chance of escaping than Saigon's. Radical anti-colonial forces had emerged in Cambodia by the early 1960s, but it was the US incursion into Cambodia in 1970 that set the country spiralling towards revolution. Until 1970 the Cambodian Communists or Khmer Rouge ("Red Cambodians") had been little more than an adjunct to the North Vietnamese troops who used eastern Cambodia as a supply route into South Vietnam, but with the extension of the fighting and the imposition of a pro-American puppet regime in Phnom Penh, the Cambodian capital, the Khmer Rouges began to fight their own liberation war, gaining support from the peasants in the countryside.

Although the North Vietnamese deported hundreds of thousands of Southerners to so-called "re-education" camps, the new rulers of Cambodia were much more radical. Their leader, Pol Pot, regarded all urban dwellers as tainted by contact with the imperialist enemy. His ultra-Maoist fundamentalism at home involved an agrarian type of communism involving emptying the cities and using mass forced labour in the countryside regardless of the human cost, which was immense. Despite wartime cooperation against the Americans, Pol Pot was virulently anti-Vietnamese and by 1978 Khmer Rouge border attacks provoked a powerful united Vietnam to invade.

Just as Pol Pot turned out not to be a Vietnamese puppet, so Hanoi turned out to be deeply suspicious of China's future ambitions in the region despite receiving military aid during the war against America. China was also a rival of Hanoi's main backer, the Soviet Union. In 1979, Vietnam invaded and quickly overran Cambodia. China then fought a short border war with Vietnam to "teach a lesson" to Hanoi but did not reverse the Vietnamese conquest of Cambodia. More than three decades of anti-colonial war against France and then America had been replaced by an even older geopolitical rivalry between Vietnam and China despite both states claiming to be communist. The communist revolution had produced profound nationalist rivalries.

A CIA employee helps Vietnamese evacuees in Saigon onto an American helicopter half a mile from the US Embassy, 29 April 1975.

Algeria 1956–62

France's defeat at Dien Bien Phu in Vietnam in 1954 not only ended her chances of holding onto her empire in Indo-China, but also encouraged rebellion in her largest remaining colony, Algeria. Under French law, Algeria was treated as part of France, though few Algerians were accorded full citizenship and voting rights. To get full citizenship, ordinary Algerians had to renounce their Muslim faith even though the French Republic was officially a secular society taking no account of its citizens' religious beliefs. Algerians began to agitate for their own statehood as other Arab and African states gained independence. There were 8.5 million of them against fewer than one million French colonists, or *pieds noirs* as they were called.

Already on 8 May 1945, the end of World War II had been marked in Algeria by a savage suppression of demonstrators calling for independence in the city of Constantine. For nine years resentment simmered and then, three months after the war in Vietnam, fighting started in Algeria on 1 November 1954, organized by the National Liberation Front (FNL), which was established by Ben Bella, an Algerian ex-soldier in the French colonial army.

In 1954, the FNL's 800 fighters fought almost 20,000 French troops. The loosely organized group relied on the backing of nine traditional chiefs across Algeria and increasingly adopted the rhetoric and structure of a modern left-wing liberation movement. Algeria's anti-colonial movement fanned into flame as countries like Egypt achieved independence and supported other North African states in the struggle for self-government. Famous anti-colonial activists, like the writer Frantz Fanon, from other parts of North Africa supported the FNL.

BRUTAL TERRORIST ATTACKS

In August 1955, the FNL launched terrorist attacks on French civilians in cities like Constantine and then the European parts of Algiers. French forces replied with atrocities of their own, even hijacking a plane carrying the FNL leader, Ben Bella, afterwards keeping him in prison until the conflict's end in 1962. Such actions generated support for the FNL and made Ben Bella a national hero.

In Algeria's key northern cities terrorism continued, with bombings of cafés used by colonists and French troops. In 1957, the

5 July 1830 French troops capture Algiers

1 November 1954 Algerian uprising begins

18 May 1958 General de Gaulle assumes power in France

1955

March 1952 Ben Bella founds National Liberation Movement (FNL)

13 May 1958 General Massu begins coup in Algiers

19 September 1958 Provisional government formed by FNL in Cairo

French authorities launched a campaign of counter-terrorism, sending the parachute forces under General Massu into the Kasbah, the Arab quarters of Algiers. Their brutal methods suppressed resistance and forced Arab civilians to reveal information about the FNL rebels. They won the battle, but their brutality outraged many French people. Writers Jean-Paul Sartre and Simone de Beauvoir organized petitions against the war. Conscripts told harrowing stories to their relatives on the mainland.

A DIVIDED FRANCE

At home the war began to divide France. After both the defeat in Vietnam and the debacle at Suez in 1956, not only communist-led left-wing forces but even some moderates began to question whether Algeria's majority could be held down by force forever. Although the news media was heavily censored in France, most knew about the war's savage nature.

After defeat in 1940 and again in 1954, the French army was determined to win. Algeria had been France's classic colony, home to the Foreign Legion and its own heroic myth. Much was at stake for France's professional soldiers who were prepared to use any means to preserve French rule. In fact, at huge cost, the French were pushing the FNL

to the margins of Algeria, but politicians at home could not stomach the price.

After the French air force's bombing of FNL bases across the Algerian border in Tunisia, the French government agreed to Anglo-American mediation of the dispute in April 1958. Convinced that the "Anglo-Saxons" would try to turn the talks into a negotiation with the rebels, in May 1958 France came close to a military coup as the army prepared to seize power to prevent any softening of the line on Algeria.

DE GAULLE LEADS NEW GOVERNMENT

General de Gaulle, the hero of resistance to Hitler, was summoned from retirement to head a new government, leading many to believe that the nationalist hard line had triumphed in Paris. However, de Gaulle had already privately recognized that France would have to make concessions. In office he came to see that the Algerian side would settle for nothing less than full independence after so much suffering.

At first the army's campaign to root out resistance in Algeria intensified. Torture became commonplace and General Massu candidly revealed to a journalist who asked about "unauthorized torture" that "there is no unauthorized torture in Algiers". Local recruits to the French security forces, the so-called *harkis*, engaged in much of the torture, making themselves doubly hated by the nationalist majority as traitors and torturers.

However, in September 1959 de Gaulle admitted that he preferred "the government of Algeria by Algerians" albeit with links to France. When he visited Algiers on 9 December 1961 de Gaulle clearly intended to loosen French control by keeping Algeria within the loose grouping of states called the French Community – the pieds noirs rioted against him for three days. De Gaulle was prepared to defy the extremists with their rallying cry of "Algerie Française" if he could chart a course for the recovery of France.

COUNTER-TERRORISM ESCALATES

De Gaulle aimed to assert French greatness while renouncing control of Algeria by funding France's first atomic bomb, tested in Algeria in February 1960. De Gaulle would renounce her colonial empire but make France a nuclear power instead.

Faced by evidence that Paris was going to abandon Algeria, pro-French extremists adopted the FLN's strategy of urban guerrilla warfare. Car bombs and tossing grenades into cafés became the tactics used by pieds

A distraught woman is comforted by a relative after losing several of her family members in the ongoing civil war, which began with an insurgency by Islamic militants in 1992.

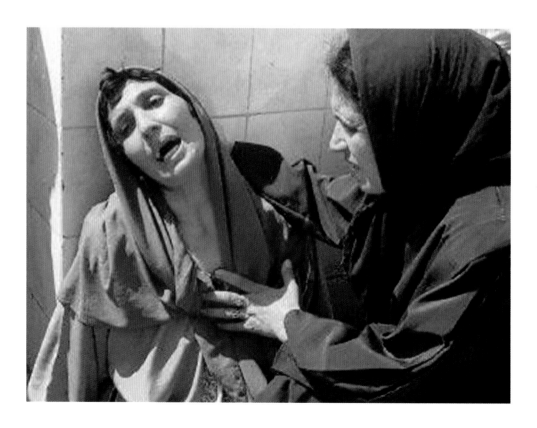

noirs and French soldiers who joined the illegal extremist movement, Organisation Armée Secrète (OAS). It targeted its terrorist attacks on both Algerian nationalists and French sympathizers, like the writer André Malraux, and even the president. OAS made several attempts to assassinate General de Gaulle, coming close to killing him in March 1962 when assassins machine-gunned his car outside Paris.

OAS COUP DEFEATED

The former French Army commander in Algeria, General Raoul Salan, organized the OAS and launched an underground campaign of terror against de Gaulle's "betrayal". Using his connections in the army, Salan staged a coup to reverse de Gaulle's plans to grant self-determination to Algeria. De Gaulle faced a dangerous balancing act for four days in April 1961 as he calmed the situation following the coup in Algiers without provoking civil war among the French or abandoning negotiations with the Algerians.

De Gaulle made excellent use of the radio. In what became the "war of transistors", the president used the new cheap means of communication to reach the mass of ordinary conscripts, persuading them to obey his orders not their superiors'.

COSTLY INDEPENDENCE

Having forestalled the generals' counter-revolution, de Gaulle still faced long and tough talks with the FNL, which recognized that the generals' defeat was a great victory for them. After the bitter conflict amassing 800,000 casualties, the FNL leaders would accept nothing less than full independence. The French economy clearly could not sustain the cost of the war.

Having defeated the attempted coup in Algeria, de Gaulle proceeded to negotiate with the FNL in the southern French spa town of Evian. It took until March 1962 for both sides to agree to a final separation. On 3 July 1962 Algeria achieved independence.

The bitter eight-year war radicalized Algerian society. The FNL envisioned a modern and socialist country that would rise out of the still largely Muslim population. As for French loyalists, scores of thousands of harkis fled to France along with 800,000 pieds noirs. Unlike the pieds noirs, the harkis did not find it easy to settle in the country and most French people wanted to turn their back on everything to do with Algeria, including the harkis.

After independence, Algeria gradually stagnated. The FNL leaders quarrelled among themselves. After his release from the French, Ben Bella was imprisoned by men who fought the war in Algeria. Secular society became corrupt and unpopular as Islam was revived in the 1980s and the FNL's heirs in the Algerian army today fight an insurrection by Muslim fundamentalists who have modelled their terrorist strategies on the FNL's successful harassment of the French before 1962.

South Africa 1980s

For almost a century after 1815, politics in what became South Africa was a struggle for control between the English-speaking arrivals and the Afrikaans-speaking Boers of Dutch-origin who had arrived during the previous century. The black majority was largely excluded and treated as people to be subjugated, or worse.

AFRIKANERS GAIN POWER

Bitter memories of the Boer War (1899–1902) for independence against Britain had made the Afrikaans-speaking whites indifferent to foreign hostility and lectures on human rights after the Second World War when South Africa bucked the trend towards anti-racism and equality elsewhere in the British Commonwealth.

Slowly but surely after South Africa received self-government from Britain in 1910, the Afrikaners gained more political power. But it was only after the Second World War, in the general election of May 1948, that their National Party won a clear majority and began to transform the existing discriminatory laws against blacks and other non-whites into the apartheid system of so-called "separate development", which not only denied non-whites the right to vote but limited where they could live, what work they could do, and banned interracial sexual relations and marriage. Families were split up, as men could only find work in South Africa's valuable mines on condition that they left their women and children confined to so-called homelands in remote and unprofitable parts of the country.

Demands for political rights by blacks had a long history. The African National Congress (ANC) had been set up in 1912, campaigning for equal rights for all inhabitants of South Africa. The ANC had followed the peaceful tactics espoused by the Indian Congress led by Mahatma Gandhi, whose political career had started in South Africa. But the triumph of the National Party in 1948, just as India and other British colonies were achieving independence, showed that South Africa was on a very different course.

Discrimination against non-white South Africans existed long before 1948. The last vestiges of black participation in the South African parliament were removed in 1936 more than a decade before apartheid became government policy. Resistance had also started before the National Party's triumph but gathered pace in the 1950s as

8 January 1912 *African National Congress (ANC) established*

May 1948 *National Party wins a clear majority*

11 June 1964 *Mandela sentenced to life imprisonment*

18 July 1918 *Birth of Nelson Mandela*

1940

21 March 1960 *Sharpeville Massacre of Black civil rights protesters by police*

the scale of apartheid's social and economic ambitions became clear. A young Xhosa lawyer, Nelson Mandela, became one of the most charismatic of the black critics of the emerging apartheid system after 1948.

MANDELA'S ARREST

By the early 1960s, Mandela had been forced to come to the conclusion that argument and protests alone would not change the white government's mind. He became involved with both the South African Communist Party and the black paramilitary group, Umkhonto we Sizwe ("Spear of the Nation"), which organized some rather amateurish attacks on power-generating facilities. Soon arrested and put on trial, Mandela's eloquent defence in court could not prevent him from receiving a life sentence, but it made an indelible mark and was widely noted around the world.

AN ALIENATED GENERATION

The chief architect of apartheid, Hendrik Verwoerd, was assassinated in 1966. But his successors left blacks and other opponents of apartheid with no political channel for their views. A few white liberals sat in the parliament but their votes carried no weight.

Despite its vast apparatus of control and repression, with a host of petty so-called

A victorious Nelson Mandela, African National Congress leader, raises his fist as he speaks to a crowded stadium in Soweto after his release from prison, 11 February 1990.

"pass laws" that humiliated non-whites, apartheid failed to reverse the growing population disparity between affluent children of white families and the economically disadvantaged booming black

17 September 1977
Black activist, Steve Biko, murdered by police

20 September 1989
FW de Klerk replaces PW Botha as President

11 February 1990 *Nelson Mandela freed from prison*

10 May 1994 *Mandela sworn in as president of South Africa*

16 June 1998 *Thabo Mbeki succeeds Mandela as president of South Africa*

16 June 1976
Beginning of schoolchildren's strike in Soweto

1990

2 February 1990 *Ban lifted on ANC*

27 April 1994 *First universal suffrage election — ANC wins 66 per cent*

9 May 1996 *New constitution adopted*

population. In the mid-1970s it was the teenage school children, who had grown up under apartheid, who revolted in the sprawling township of Soweto, exemplifying the alienation of the coming generation.

SANCTIONS WEAKEN ECONOMY

Relying on their country's value to the West because of its vast mineral, gold, and diamond wealth plus its strategic position at Africa's tip, the National Party government thought that a white-ruled South Africa would ride out the changes that toppled even Portuguese colonial rule in Angola and Mozambique to their north, and led white-ruled Rhodesia to accept black-majority rule as Zimbabwe in 1980.

By the late 1980s, anti-apartheid movements had already persuaded many US and European countries to disinvest in the South African economy rather than face boycotts at home and the end of the Cold War removed lingering US and West European support for apartheid South Africa. The country had lost its valuable strategic position protecting key trade routes, especially for Western oil tankers around the Cape of Good Hope, and Western politicians who had previously soft-pedalled sanctions against the country saw little reason to block them once the Soviet bloc dissolved.

After years of living beneath the oppressive shadow of apartheid, high-school students riot in a Soweto street near Winnie Mandela's house, 1986.

MANDELA INAUGURATED

The National Party recognized the winds of change and replaced the hard-line President P W Botha with the more amenable F W de Klerk in 1989, who pushed ahead talks with the ANC. In February 1990, Nelson Mandela was released from prison. Before his release he had been treated with special respect by the regime, and P W Botha himself had visited him to try to persuade him to renounce any support for the liberation struggle as a precondition for release. De Klerk set Mandela free without conditions.

A difficult four-year period of negotiations followed Mandela's release. Hardliners tried to provoke conflict between black tribes, setting the Zulus of Natal against the ANC-supporting Xhosas. Meanwhile Mandela's marriage to Winnie fell apart with reports of her adultery and her use of terror against critics. However, Mandela and De Klerk agreed to a peaceful resolution by setting the date for the first universal suffrage elections in South Africa on 27 April 1994, which led to Mandela's inauguration as the country's first black head of state.

Given past bitterness, the agreement was remarkable. A key difference between the ANC and other liberation movements in Africa was that it did not deny South Africa's legitimacy as a state or the whites' right to be there. It wanted full political rights for the majority of the population but was not anti-colonial in the same way that in Algeria, for instance, independence had meant the expulsion of the French settlers.

To the surprise of some, the elections did not eliminate the National Party. In the Western Cape its local leaders targeted the large coloured and Asian population, played on fears of black majority rule, and won a narrow majority. It may not have been pretty but it provided a pragmatic counterbalance to the ANC's overall two-thirds majority, which helped to reassure whites.

South Africa tried to overcome its bitter and divisive past by using a "truth commission" chaired by Archbishop Tutu to allow those responsible for violent acts on both sides to set the record straight with testimony in return for amnesty. Only ex-President P W Botha refused to cooperate and the state was slow to prosecute such a relic of what now seemed a bygone age.

Mandela's extraordinary popularity among all racial groups could not be transferred to his successor, Thabo Mbeki, and politics as usual returned after Mandela's retirement in 1998. Mbeki, who had spent much of his adulthood outside South Africa, faced challenges from internal ANC activists. The challenge for South Africa after the transition to majority rule was how to tackle the vast residual problems of economic inequality inherited from apartheid. A few blacks have entered the privileged elite, but Mandela's successors face the severe challenge of satisfying their vast poor black constituency without undermining the white-run economy. It is the classic challenge to would-be peaceful revolutionaries: can they continue to promote large-scale change without provoking a crisis?

Key Figures

Bin Laden, Osama
Born the 7th son of a wealthy Saudi construction magnate in 1957, Osama Bin Laden took part in the anti-Soviet struggle in Afghanistan after 1984. He turned against his former US sponsors in 1991 when American troops came to Saudi Arabia to fight neighbouring Iraq. After several years of exile in Sudan, Bin Laden found refuge in Afghanistan in 1996. With other militant Arab exiles he established bases for the Islamic fundamentalist Al Qaeda (Citadel) movement in cooperation with the Taliban regime. In 1998 US cruise missiles attacked these bases in reprisal for Al Qaeda bombings of American embassies in Kenya and Tanzania. After the 11th September 2001 attacks on New York and Washington, Bin Laden's base in Afghanistan became the object of a massive US attack.

Bolivar, Simón (1783–1830) Born into a wealthy Venezuelan Creole family, Bolivar became the most prominent champion of independence for Spain's Latin American colonies after 1808.

Castro, Fidel (1927–) Cuban guerrilla leader and communist head of state. Fidel Castro was attracted to radical politics and resented US domination of Cuba. After a period in Mexican exile in 1956, he established himself as a guerrilla leader, coming to power in 1959. In 1961, Castro took the post of Prime Minister, which he held until 1976 when he became President.

Ceausescu, Nicolae (1918–1989) Romanian Communist Party leader since 1965, Ceausescu was overthrown and shot in the most dramatic of the 1989 revolutions.

Cromwell, Oliver (1599–1658) A member of Parliament from 1640–1653, Cromwell led the New Model Army for Parliament in the Civil War, 1644–43. He signed the death-warrant of Charles I in 1649, seized political power in 1653, and was named Lord Protector of Britain, 1654–58.

De Valera, Eammon (1882–1975) De Valera played a leading role in the Easter Uprising of 1916 and was elected leader of Sinn Fein in 1917. He led the anti-Free State side in the Irish civil war but accepted the new state in 1926, serving as Irish premier from 1932–48 and again in the 1950s. De Valera steered the creation of the "Irish Republic", and was president from 1959 until 1973.

Franco, Francisco (1892–1975) A Spanish general who led the military coup against the Republic in July 1936, Franco consolidated his position as Caudillo after victory in 1939. He survived Hitler and Mussolini to rule until 1975.

Guevara, Ernesto "Che" (1928–1967) An Argentinian-born revolutionary activist who became the world's most photogenic guerrilla after his participation in the Cuban revolution, 1959. After serving as a minister in Cuba until 1965, Che went to Bolivia in the hope of fomenting a similar revolution there but instead he was captured and executed – a martyrdom which gave him mythic status.

Hitler, Adolf (1889–1945) Born in Austria, Hitler joined the German Army in 1914, became active in radical right-wing politics in Germany after 1919, and was imprisoned for his putsch attempt in 1923. A member of the German Reichstag (parliament) from 1924–33, he was appointed chancellor in January 1933, centralizing power in his own hands the following year. Hitler launched the Second World War on September 1939 but eventually committed suicide before inevitable defeat by the Allies in April 1945.

Ho Chi Minh (1890–1969) Born in French Indo-China, Ho came to Europe before the World War I and helped found the French Communist Party. Returning to the Far East via Moscow, he worked with Chinese communists to overthrow Japanese rule before returning to his native Vietnam in 1943. Ho led the anti-French liberation struggle from 1945–1954 and was leader of North Vietnam until his death.

Jefferson, Thomas (1743–1826) The main author of US Declaration of Independence in 1776, Jefferson served as US president from 1801–09.

Khomeini, Ayatollah Rhullah (1902–1989) Fundamentalist Shiite Muslim cleric whose challenges to the Shah's westernizing regime led to his exile from Iran in 1964. He returned in triumph in February 1979, and remained a dominant political and religious figure until his death in 1989.

Kun, Bela (1886–1939) Leader of the short-lived Hungarian Soviet Republic in 1919, Kun fled to the Soviet Union where he fell foul of Stalin's purges as an exile.

Lenin, Vladimir Ilich Ulyanov (1870–1924) The son of a government official, Lenin became a Marxist activist and leader of the majority ("Bolshevik") wing of the Russian Social Democratic Party in 1902. He lived in exile in Switzerland but returned to Russia in April 1917, leading the communist revolution in November. He led the government, 1917–24, though hampered by illness in his final years.

Luxemburg, Rosa (1871–1919) Polish-Jewish by origin, Luxemburg became a Marxist activist who was a key figure in the radical wing of the German Social Democratic Party opposing participation in World War I (with Karl Liebknecht 1871–1919). She was murdered on 15 January 1919.

Mandela, Nelson (1918–) From a relatively privileged Black South African family, Mandela was educated as a lawyer as the ruling white minority was establishing the apartheid system. From 1952, Mandela was a civil rights activist, deciding in 1961 that only force could overthrow the South African regime. Imprisoned from 1963 until 1990, Mandela became apartheid's symbolic victim and huge campaigns for his release were organized around the world. After his release in 1990, Mandela helped negotiate the transition to the first one person-one vote elections in 1994, which led to his own election as President of South Africa, a post he held until 1999.

Mao Zedong (1893–1976) Born in Hunan in 1893, Mao Zedong was one of the founders of the Chinese Communist Party in 1921. As architect of the Party's successful guerrilla campaigns against the Nationalist regime and the Japanese invaders (1931–45), Mao became the model for Third World Revolutionaries. After taking power in 1949, Mao's autocratic personality led him into conflict with other Communist leaders as he pressed for radical policies and purged the Party in the Cultural Revolution.

Mussolini, Benito (1883–1945) Born into a poor Italian family, largely self-educated, and a formidable Socialist journalist and politician, Mussolini suddenly denounced his old pacifism and radicalism to become an advocate of Italian entry into the World War I in 1914. Afterwards he established the first fascist movement and developed the new style of demagogic dictatorship imitated by Hitler in Germany.

Nagy, Imre 1896–1958) The Hungarian communist leader's political commitment began as a prisoner-of-war in revolutionary Russia after 1917. After Soviet occupation of Hungary in 1945, he became Minister of Justice during the purge period (1948–53), but belonged to the reform wing of Party leadership after Stalin's death. In October 1956 Nagy became premier during the revolution and agreed to radical anti-Soviet steps. After Soviet troops occupied Hungary, Nagy was executed and secretly buried in 1958.

Omar, Mullah Mohammed
Born in 1957 in Noudi near Kandahar, Mohammed Omar was still training to be an Islamic cleric when the Soviet invasion of Afghanistan turned him into a "holy warrior". He lost an eye fighting the Russians but it was only after he organised a group of religious students (Taliban) in 1994 to stop rape and pillage in his home region that Mullah Omar became a political figure. Within two years his

movement had swept to power in Kabul though he remained in Kandahar where wrapped in the Prophet Mohammed's cloak he was proclaimed Emir. His support for Osama Bin Laden's international Islamic terror group, Al Qaeda, brought the wrath of America down on Taliban Afghanistan in 2001 and his regime was shattered in two months. Even Mullah Omar himself ignored his own appeals to die a martyr's death rather than surrender.

Orange, William Prince of (1533–1584) One of the greatest landowners in the Netherlands, William of Orange renounced his Catholic religion and loyalty to the Habsburg dynasty to lead the struggle for religious freedom and political liberation after 1568. Assassinated in 1584 by a pro-Spanish friar, William of Orange was the leading figure in the new bourgeois Dutch Republic.

Robespierre, Maximilien (1758–1794) This French lawyer became one of the most radical republicans after 1789. Originally an opponent of the death penalty, he became a leading proponent of the Terror from 1793–94, but lost popular support in the summer of 1794 and was himself guillotined.

Soares, Mario (1924–) Lisbon-born and -educated lawyer, Soares tried to oppose the Salazar regime but was forced into exile in 1969. He returned after the April 1974 revolution and led the moderate Socialist Party opposing the more radical pro-Soviet elements in Portuguese politics. Prime Minister twice (1976–78 and 1983–85) He was President of Portugal from 1986–1995.

Trotsky, Leon Bronstein (1879–1940) Born into a Jewish family in the Ukraine and already a revolutionary by the age of 20. At first he opposed Lenin's Bolsheviks but later joined them in 1917. He was Soviet Russia's first foreign commissar in charge of peace negotiations, 1917–18, and then organized the Red Army in the Russian Civil War, 1918–20. An advocate of "permanent revolution" after Lenin's death, Trotsky lost power to Stalin, was exiled in 1929, and murdered in Mexico by Stalin's agent in 1940.

Washington, George (1732–1799) Commander of the Continental Army in the American Revolution against British rule (1774–83), Washington was the first President of the United States of America (1789–97).

William III (1650–1702) Born Prince of Orange, William III married Mary, the Protestant daughter of England's Catholic king, James II, and invaded England in 1688 at the invitation of Protestant grandees, who feared James II's Catholicizing policies. As joint monarch with his wife after 1689, William III was the guarantor of the "Glorious Revolution" until his death in 1702.

Yeltsin, Boris (1931–) First post-Soviet leader of Russia. Born in Siberia, Yeltsin rose through the Communist Party from party boss in his native Sverdlovsk (now Ekaterinburg) to join Mikhail Gorbachev's politburo in 1985 and Moscow City Communist leader until 1987, when he fell out with the other communist leaders. In 1989 he made a comeback winning Moscow's seat in the new Congress of People's Deputies. In June 1991, he was the first directly elected President of still Soviet Russia and that August played a key role facing down the anti-Gorbachev hardline coup. In December 1991, Yeltsin sealed the break-up of the Soviet Union by becoming president of an independent Russia. Although re-elected in 1996, years of alcoholism had undermined his health and the prematurely aged Yeltsin dramatically resigned on New Year's Eve 1999.

Zapata, Emiliano (1879–1919) A charismatic mestizo from Morelos, Zapata took up the cause of landless Indians against the great landowners and joined the rebellion against President Díaz in 1910 only to be abandoned by the revolutionary leaders after victory and treacherously murdered in 1919.

Index

Figures in italics refer to captions.

Acknowledgments

I would like to thank Vivien Antwi, who first proposed the project to me, Michelle Bernard, Lindsay Porter and Mark Fletcher at Mitchell Beazley for their patience with an author whose broken ankle in Belgrade was only one of many frustrations in bringing this book to fruition.

Bibliography

Dunn, John. *Modern Revolutions: An Introduction to the Analysis of a Political Phenomenon.* Cambridge: Cambridge University Press, 1989.

Goldstone, Jack A. *Revolution and Rebellion in the Early Modern World.* Berkeley: University of California Press, 1991.

Kimmel, Michael S. *Revolution: A Sociological Interpretation.* Cambridge: Polity Press, 1990.

Krejci, Jaroslav. *Great Revolutions Compared: The Outline of a Theory.* Hemel Hempstead: Harvester Wheatsheaf Press, 1994.

Linz, Juan J and Stepan, Alfred. *Problems of Democratic Transition and Consolidation: Southern Europe, South America, and Post-Communist Europe.* Baltimore: Johns Hopkins University Press, 1996.

Skocpol, Theda. *States & Social Revolutions: A Comparative Analysis of France, Russia & China.* Cambridge: Cambridge University Press, 1979.

Tocqueville, Alexis de. *The Old Order and the Revolution,* Edited with an introduction by François Furet and Françoise Mélonio, trans. Alan S Kahan. Chicago: Chicago University Press, 1998.

Walt, Stephen M. *Revolution and War.* Ithaca: Cornell University Press, 1996.

Picture Credits

Front cover Popperfoto
Back cover Bridgeman Art Library/Musèe de la Ville de Paris/Musèe Carnavalet/Lauros-Giraudon

2 Popperfoto/Reuters/Petar Kujundzic; 7 AKG, London; 11 Agence France Presse; 13 Novosti; 15 Kobal Collection/UFA; 18 AKG, London/Erich Lessing/Mauritshuis, The Hague; 23 AKG, London; 24 Bridgeman Art Library/Leeds Museums and Galleries (City Art Gallery) UK; 27 Bridgeman Art Library/Trinity College, Cambridge; 28 Bridgeman Art Library/Metropolitan Museum of Art, New York; 31 Hulton Archive; 33 AKG, London/Private Collection; 36 AKG, London; 38-39 Hulton Archive; 41 AKG, London; 42 Novosti (London); 45 Novosti (London); 46-47 Hulton Archive; 49 AKG, London; 50 AKG, London; 53 Hulton Archive; 54-55 AKG, London; 58 Sally and Richard Greenhill; 61 Corbis UK Ltd/Bettmann; 62 Corbis UK Ltd/Bettmann; 65 Hulton Archive; 67 Associated Press Ltd/Stringer; 71 Popperfoto; 73 Corbis UK Ltd/David Turnley; 74 Corbis UK Ltd/Bettmann; 77 Corbis UK Ltd/Bettmann; 79 AKG, London; 80 Kobal Collection/Mosfilm; 83 Corbis UK Ltd; 86-87 Corbis UK Ltd/Sergio Dorantes; 89 AKG, London/Erich Lessing; 92 Popperfoto; 95 AKG, London; 96 Corbis UK Ltd/(c)Reuters Newmedia Inc; 99 Hulton Archive; 100 Rex Features; 103 Agence France Presse/Edgar Romero; 107 Agence France Presse/Politikens Pressfoto; 108 Corbis UK Ltd/Owen Franken; 111 Corbis UK Ltd/David & Peter Turnley; 112 Novosti (London); 116 Popperfoto; 119 Corbis UK Ltd/Bettmann; 121 Corbis UK Ltd; 125 Roger-Viollet/Harlingue-Viollet; 127 AKG, London/Civiche Raccolte d'Arte, Milano; 128 Hulton Archive; 131 Corbis UK Ltd/c Archivio Iconogrfico, SA; 132 AKG, London; 137 Corbis UK Ltd/(c) Reuters Newmedia Inc; 138 Corbis UK Ltd/c Bettmann; 141 Popperfoto /Claudia Daut, Reuters; 143 Popperfoto; 146 Corbis UK Ltd/Bettmann; 149 Corbis UK Ltd/Peter Turnley; 151 Corbis UK Ltd/Contemporary African Art Collection; 155 Jon Arnold Images; 156 RMN/A Danvers/Musèe des Beaux-Arts, Bordeaux; 159 Bridgeman Art Library/Musèe de la Ville de Paris, Musèe Carnavalet/ Lauros-Giraudon; 160 Hulton Archive; 165 Kobal Collection/Geffen /Warner Bros; 167 Agence France Presse/Intercontinentale; 168 Popperfoto; 171 Corbis UK Ltd/Bettmann; 174 Agence France Presse; 177 Corbis UK Ltd/Peter Turnley; 178 Corbis UK Ltd/David Turnley.